MIXED BLESSINGS

Simple Pleasures

To Joni,

You have been a long time,
faithful friend who has helped
me, encouraged me, and laughed
with me as we've both experienced
triumphs & tragedies in our
Christian walk.

You have been a diamond
in my life, Joni.

May God bless you, always.

With love

Marilee

BREATH OF FRESH AIR PRESS

Mixed Blessings— Simple Pleasures
Published by Breath of Fresh Air Press
PO Box 12, St Clair NSW 2759
Australia
www.breathoffreshairpress.com.au

© 2014 Breath of Fresh Air Press

ISBN: 978-1-922135-00-1 (paperback)

Unless otherwise indicated, Scripture quotations are taken from THE HOLY BIBLE, NEW INTERNATIONAL VERSION®, NIV® Copyright © 1973, 1978, 1984, 2011 by Biblica, Inc.® Used by permission. All rights reserved worldwide.

Scripture quotations taken from the 21st Century King James Version®, copyright © 1994. Used by permission of Deuel Enterprises, Inc., Gary, SD 57237. All rights reserved.

Scripture taken from the NEW AMERICAN STANDARD BIBLE®, Copyright © 1960,1962,1963, 1968,1971,1972,1973,1975,1977,1995 by The Lockman Foundation. Used by permission.

National Library of Australia Cataloguing-in-Publication entry
Title: Mixed blessings : simple pleasures /
                    compiled and edited by Deborah Porter ; Jan Ackerson, editor ;
                    Steve Ariss, cover design
ISBN: 9781922135001 (paperback)
Subjects: Short stories
                   Poetry
                   Christian life in literature
Other Authors/Contributors:
                   Porter, Deborah Ann, compiler, editor.
                   Ackerson, Jan, editor.
                   Ariss, Steve.
Dewey Number: A823.01

Compiled by: Deborah Porter
Editors: Deborah Porter, Finesse Writing & Editing Service (Australia)
                 Jan Ackerson, Superior Editing Services (United States)
Cover Design: Steve Ariss, Arissberg.com
Layout: Breath of Fresh Air Press

Introduction

"Come to me, all you who are weary and burdened,
and I will give you rest"
Matthew 11:28

*L*IFE IN THE 21ST CENTURY is hyper-busy and time-poor, and this in spite of the abundance of labor and time-saving devices at our disposal. Seriously, it would boggle my brain . . . if my brain had the time to waste thinking about such things.

Surely "time saving" should actually mean there is a stash of hours and minutes tucked away, preferably accruing a good rate of interest. Unfortunately, even if such a time savings account existed, I suspect my account would be heavily overdrawn.

It is a conundrum—time, time everywhere, but not a second to spare.

Sound familiar? You aren't alone.

With the pace of everyday life increasing at a mind-blowing rate, and the constant pressure to be the perfect employee, spouse, parent, friend, church member (add your own area of unattainable perfection), we all need to find ways to escape and be refreshed, even if only for an hour or two, or perhaps a few brief moments in a hectic day.

Simple pleasures are all around us, waiting to be noticed and enjoyed. In fact, as I write, I can see one right outside my window. My home office looks out on a postage stamp size lawn enclosed by a curved garden wall, filled with flowering shrubs and trees. It is a delight, but a delight I rarely stop to experience. Oh, but when I do, what joy.

A shaft of sunlight through the office blinds invites me to set aside my work for a moment, step outside and stand still in the center of the lawn, absorbing the sounds and scents of this little slice of creation. Then, as I wait in the stillness, an extra gift arrives in the form of butterflies, flittering and floating in the air around me. A mere five minutes in this little garden, kissed by the sun and embraced by butterflies, is enough to bring a smile to my face and a reminder that life is so much more than work and deadlines.

My simple pleasures may not be the same as yours, but we all have little things that brighten our day. Going outside to throw a ball around may be the perfect recharge for you. Or perhaps a trip to the mall is the ideal pick-me-up. Maybe baking a batch of cookies or reading a book leaves you feeling good. In this world of technological marvels, I find comfort in the knowledge that we don't really need all the gadgets and gizmos to find contentment (regardless of what the advertising gurus may tell us).

With that thought in mind, we challenged a large group of Christian writers at FaithWriters.com to let their creativity loose with ten fun topics representing a variety of life's simplest pleasures. To make things interesting, we did not reveal the theme, allowing these talented writers plenty of room to explore each activity in unusual ways, adding their own surprising twists and turns. Over the course of ten weeks, we received over 1,500 submissions, and the very best of all those articles are contained in this book.

Mixed Blessings—Simple Pleasures is a perfect blend of one hundred stories, articles, and poems, by over fifty talented writers, each bringing their own unique view and, quite often, surprising depth of meaning and interpretation to these otherwise everyday activities. As with all *Mixed Blessings* books, there really is something for every Christian reader. An abundance of smiles, tears, encouragement, inspiration, and food for thought packed into every book.

With such diversity of talent and creative interpretation, perhaps the simplest pleasure of all is the book you are holding right now. So, take a break from all the activities and work of your busy day, sit back, relax, and be refreshed.

Deb Porter
Writing Challenge Coordinator
FaithWriters.com

Table of Contents

PART FOUR: CRAFTED WITH LOVE

PART FIVE: SHOP TILL YOU DROP

PART SIX: PUTTING PEN TO PAPER

PART TEN: MAKE A JOYFUL NOISE

PART ONE

Something's Cooking

Fanning the Flame

Corinne Smelker

DEAR MOTHER,
I appreciate you sending the fire trucks last night after my panicked call to you, but really, everything is fine. The assessor says the damage to the house is not all that bad, and he thinks he can get our insurance to pay for it with little trouble. He did say he may "fudge" his report a tad, more to protect the innocent than to defraud the insurance company, for which Frank shall be eternally grateful!

You see, Mother, Frank decided to make one of his rare forays into my domain—AKA the kitchen—to make, in his words, a "slap up dinner."

Immediately, I placed the kids on red alert because we all know what happened the last time he cooked. Although I heard recently from the campground manager that the burnt patch is growing back, and they were able to rescue some of the rarer plants.

Anyway, I digress . . .

Frank pulled out steaks and turned on the gas for oil to fry some chips. He was admonishing me for not believing in him enough when the cat entered the kitchen. Never have I seen a cat lurk so effectively as Blackie. Personally, I think he was shocked to see Frank in so strange a place. He's used to curling up on Frank's lap as they watch BBC at night.

Frank told me what happened next, as I was out in the garden enjoying a cup of tea at the time.

He had just pulled the oil off the stove when Blackie darted between his legs (to get a closer look, I think). Down Frank went, holding onto the pan, but the oil still managed to slop all over the floor.

Thank God for small mercies, it missed Blackie.

Oh, and it missed Frank too.

But some of it splashed up and hit the gas flame, which flared. Not thinking, Frank grabbed the nearest thing, which was Blackie, and was about to use him to beat out the flames.

Blackie didn't take kindly to being an extinguisher and scratched Frank quite effectively up and down both arms before clawing at his legs and making his escape.

(The Casualty Department said Frank should be all right. They administered an anti-tetanus shot and told Frank the scratches should not scar too badly.)

Why Frank didn't call out to me, I will never know!

He also didn't think to turn the gas off, so by then the flames were several feet high. A sudden gust of wind caused one of my curtains to flap over the flame, and before Frank knew it, the curtains were both on fire.

Unbeknownst to me, Frank was on the floor, writhing in agony from the injuries inflicted on him by poor Blackie, and my kitchen was merrily going up in smoke.

The first clue I had that something was wrong was when Mrs. Robinson from next door came outside to fetch her wash. "Wotcha cooking?" she asked.

"Nothing."

"Well, you could have fooled me. Have you looked behind you lately?"

I turned around and all I could see was smoke pouring out the open kitchen window. Mother, I have never run so fast in all my life!

Blackie darted past me as I ran in, giving me an "I'm never coming back here" look. Frank was still prone on the kitchen floor, and the flames had engulfed the stove and my curtains and were happily making their way to my kitchen table.

I yelled for the kids and together we hauled Frank to safety. Then I tried dousing the fire with water. That's when I called you.

The fire trucks got here pretty quickly, and as I said, the assessor said the damage was not too bad. Thank God.

He did ask what we should put down as the cause of the accident, but told me "stupidity in the kitchen" does not count. After some consultation, Frank and I have decided to leave Blackie out of the equation and go for simple "fat fire" for insurance purposes. I have assured Frank his secret is safe with me.

Well . . . me, the firemen, the assessor, you, Mrs. Robinson . . .

We plan on coming to see you next month, and Frank mentioned that he wants to make his world famous bangers and mash while visiting, but I just said "Blackie," and he kept quiet.

With love from your daughter,

Doris

Apricot Pie Memories

MARTY WELLINGTON

THE TINY KANSAS FARMHOUSE seemed to sway against a mighty prairie wind. I could hear every creak and heave of its wooden frame as I paced around Grandma's tiny kitchen. The cracked linoleum floor was a minefield for those not wearing shoes. Thankfully, I had remembered to slip on wool socks and my Birks.

I looked around the kitchen, attempting to get my bearings after many years' absence. Whisperings of a little girl's giggles and a Grandma's cooking lessons wrapped me in a warm embrace. A scuffling noise from deeper in the house interrupted my thoughts.

"Sarah, is that you? You're up already?"

I recognized my mother's sleepy voice approaching down the hallway.

"Yeah. Just looking around, thinking, wondering."

As Mom drew closer, I could see the grief in her eyes, her sagging shoulders. For the first time, I really wondered what it would be like to lose a parent . . . to lose her someday. Grandma had just died. Tomorrow was her funeral. Somehow, we all had to deal with this new emptiness in our lives, but no one more so than my mother. I reached out to her, hugging her tightly around the waist, attempting to share some of her burden. She slumped against me. Roles were suddenly reversed, and I was the comforter, mothering her.

It was in that moment I knew what I must do for myself, my mother, and my grandmother—pay homage to the cooking legacy Grandma Louise had left here in this small country kitchen. "Mom, let's make pies."

She responded with a weak smile, her blue eyes tired and lifeless. "I've never been the pie baker, Sarah. You know that."

"Don't worry. I'll do most of the work. We need to do this for Grandma." I looked her straight in the eye. "For us."

She nodded.

After a pseudo breakfast of water and granola bars, Mom began inventorying ingredients while I assembled dishes and explored the worn-out cabinets. It was easy to get lost in the mountains of musty Tupperware and brightly colored glass dishes. There were so many memories of spilled flour and sweet-tasting pastries. My mind conjured up images from the orchard—picking ripe tart cherries, golden apricots, and juicy peaches. And, of course, the sweet scent of fresh baked pies.

Grandma's era of cooking had its roots in necessity and provision for her family, yet her dedication to her craft had translated into wonderful hobbies for Mom and me—lessons and habits we cherished. I've often wondered if baking is hereditary; it definitely is in our family.

"Well, the flour has weevils, there's no butter or cinnamon . . . and I hate to think how old this sugar is. It's crusty. You know it's been years since Mom . . . your Grandma baked."

"You better just pitch everything and I'll make a run to the grocery store downtown. Don't worry, Mom. We'll get it done."

That afternoon, Mom and I worked together, memories swirling around the kitchen much like the cream cheese in Grandma's pumpkin bread. We laughed, we cried, we hugged, but most importantly, we baked—and not just pies. Nut breads, and rolls, and crusty peasant bread topped with herbs and sea salt. All to honor a lady who shared her life and her love with us.

While it was Mom's intent to share the baked goods at the funeral dinner, I had other ideas for one special apricot pie—Grandma's favorite.

The morning of her funeral, the Kansas winds shrieked and howled like prairie coyotes. With all the commotion, I worried that I would wake Mom as I tiptoed through the old farmhouse, trying to avoid the inevitable squeaky floorboards.

The apricot pie glistened on the sideboard. I scooped it up and rushed out the door, making my way downtown to the funeral home. When I arrived, the funeral director gave me a quizzical look, but with the kindness and enthusiasm so indicative of men in his position, he placed a beautiful Romanesque wood column at the head of Grandma's casket. It served to display my tribute to Grandma—a handmade apricot pie.

Grandma would be proud.

Nothing Left

PAT GUY

*S*HE WAS DYING AND she knew it. Emaciated and weak, she cleared the dust from her lungs.

It was everywhere. The slightest movement of her sandals stirred parched land beneath her feet. It was dying, too. Oppressive heat moved throughout the city, looking for those ready to succumb to this drought. Not many could hold out much longer.

She could see deep into the blue of the sky that day, like the many days before it, and just as empty were her jars at home.

Why did I come to this gate? It was foolish to walk so far to gather these few sticks for a meal that could not feed one, let alone two.

But something had drawn her this way. Her son—her precious, precious . . .

Oh, my son! I despair at the sight of your flesh that clings to your bones. Oh, that I could give of my life to sustain yours. My heart is in anguish for you, my son, my precious, precious son.

Tears disappeared quickly into withered cheeks and wrinkled palms. Sticks fell from her grasp and tumbled to the cracked earth along the city wall. She slid down its support as legs gave way and soul no longer had the strength to stand.

The mournful sway of her body caught the attention of a man. An observer would say his intent was to walk in her direction as though he had purpose of her, but she took no notice. Despair is like that. One cannot see beyond its thick black veil.

He called to her. "Would you bring me a little water in a jar so that I may have a drink?"[1]

She looked up at this stranger who shielded her from the sun. His attire was that of a prophet, but it was more than his apparel that drew her to her feet. The same urgency she had felt to come to this gate now drew her to fulfill this prophet's request. She lowered her eyes and left; the snap of brittle wood as she walked away her only reply.

He called to her once again. "And bring me, please, a piece of bread."[2]

Her shoulders dropped with a sigh too heavy to hold and she turned to face this impossible demand. "As surely as the Lord your God lives," she replied, "I do not have any bread—only a handful of flour in a jar and a little oil in a jug. I was gathering a few sticks to take home and make a meal for myself and my son that we may eat it—and die."[3]

What more could this prophet ask? There was nothing left. Even their lives would soon be gone.

"Do not be afraid," the prophet said.

The woman held on to the wall. *'Do not be afraid?' I am terrified!*

"Go home and do as you have said. But first make a small cake of bread for me from what you have."

Sacrifice my son for a man I do not know? I cannot do this!

"Then make something for yourself and your son," he continued.

Is this a mockery of our lives? To give all, only to have nothing left . . . but death?

Her gaze did not waver from his. She searched for something, anything, in his eyes.

He spoke to her silent plea. "For this is what the Lord, the God of Israel, says; 'The jar of flour will not be used up and the jug of oil will not run dry until the day the Lord gives rain on the land.'"[4]

Sealed with assurance, she went away and did what the prophet, Elijah, told her. She baked all she had left and served Elijah the meager cake of bread while her starving son watched and kept an eye on the stranger. All the while, the woman smiled calm assurance.

She gathered his thin body into her loving arms and whispered close to his ear, "My son, my son . . . my precious, precious son. Go look into the jar of flour and lift the jug of oil. It is time now for a feast."

Empty had been made full . . . with life.

~~⌇⟡⌇~~

Based on the story from 1Kings 17:7-15

[1] 1Kings 17:10
[2] 1Kings 17:11
[3] 1Kings 17:12
[4] 1Kings 17:14

A Life Like Chicken and Dumplings

DEBORA DYESS

"IT'S CHICKEN AND DUMPLINGS night," Mona informed Chanelle as the girl entered the kitchen. "Know how to make them?"

Chanelle nodded. "Boil the chicken and dump biscuits in there."

"Well, that's one way." Mona smiled at her new foster daughter. "My way's a little more complicated, but it turns out better in the long run. Either way is okay, but if you put in a few extra ingredients and take your time, it's really good."

"Okay." The girl shrugged. "What do you need me to do?"

Each child in the household, whether they were foster, visitor, or blood-related, took a turn cooking. Tonight would be Chanelle's first time. She'd been in the house for only a week, and Mona knew the girl felt like an outsider.

"I'll tell you some stuff to get out," Mona said, pulling an apron around her T-shirt and jeans. "We'll work on this together."

Chanelle gathered items as Mona called them out. "Onion, garlic, celery, a stick of butter, a can of milk, flour . . . oh, and a cup of hot tea for each of us."

At the table, Mona crushed a bulb of garlic while Chanelle chopped an onion. After a while, the girl paused. "Why all this work?" she asked. "It's just chicken and dumplings."

Mona smiled. "Soup is like life. You get out of it what you put into it."

"What d'you mean?"

"Do you remember the sermon at church on Sunday morning?"

Chanelle nodded, although she'd dozed through part of it. Sunday had been her first time in a church since her grandmother's death five years before, and sitting still that long just didn't come easy for the girl.

"He talked about . . . um . . . about, like . . . Jesus . . . and us?"

Mona tried to stifle a grin and Chanelle giggled.

"He talked about life, Mona said. "He talked about how God gives us all life but wants to give us more. God wants us to have abundant life through his son, Jesus." She finished chopping the celery and took a sip of tea. "Sounds easy. Just live a life and do well. But it's kind of like this chicken and dumpling recipe.

There's a lot more to it than most people realize. There's a lot of work to it. Why, for this recipe you have to make a roux out of flour and butter, get the broth to just the right temperature and whisk it in, boil the vegetables until they are the right softness, add some milk at the right time . . . it's anything but boiling a chicken and stirring in biscuits. But, oh," Mona smiled, "the smell and taste when you're done."

She stood from the table and walked over to the stove, carefully adding the vegetables to the simmering stock. "It's worth every minute of trouble, every penny spent on ingredients, every bit of extra work."

"And that's like life, huh?"

Mona nodded. "That's what Dan and I would like to show you, Chanelle. A life that's different. A life that's so far above the average that you wonder how other people survive without having what you have."

Chanelle leaned against the countertop, frowning. "Yeah, until I mess up. Then I'm kind of like this onion." She poured it into the pot. "Done."

Mona looked into Chanelle's dark, troubled eyes. "No, ma'am." She laid the spoon down and took her foster child by the hands. "We figure you're worth the trouble, too. We're going to spend the time, and the pennies, and the work, and whatever else it takes to help you become everything God has for you. We're going to do everything we can to show you that abundant life."

Chanelle wiped at the tears that welled in her eyes. She reached for the large wooden spoon and stirred the contents of the pot. "Kind of like chicken and dumplings?"

Mona smiled. "Exactly like chicken and dumplings."

The Devil's Stew

LINDA WATSON OWEN

The Devil stirred a boiling stew
And cackled in the night.
His devious recipe and brew
Were giving him delight!
His eyes aflame and watering mouth
Hung over his dread pot
As in his mind a sickening sauce
Now simmered his foul plot.

"I'll stir their souls in hellion broth.
Oh, how their sins will flow!
They'll think they're in a pleasure pond.
Ha ha! They'll never know
That like a frog, the heat will rise
And still they'll smile and sing
Until the boiling point is met.
Then I'll own everything!"

The Devil counted out the cups
Of *Have Yourself Some Fun*
And tossed them in the cauldron,
Quite enough for everyone.
"I'll add a spoonful of *Get Rich*,
A pinch of *Want it Now*,
One whiff of this and they'll be mine.
Chef Sin will take a bow."

So through the night this ornery wretch
Stirred on in giggling glee,
Elated by the bubbling batch
Of broth so thickening sweet.
And by the light of lapping flames
That licked the slopping rim
The Devil added one more BAM!
Of *Who Cares Where I've Been.*

The brewing mess smelled sugary,
A treat for any tongue,
especially for those adrift
Or for the very young.
You'd think the dark would give a clue
This is no place to be,
But as he planned, the great pot's heat
Increased by each degree.

No soul jumped out or took a note
That something was amiss.
Instead they swam and drank the soup
of clueless naughty bliss.
Again the Devil cackled loud
Into the moonlit skies,
But little did he know it then.
He didn't realize.

The very skies that echoed back
His laughter so depraved
Would in that same night open for
The One Who comes to save.
A blinding light! A trumpet blast!
A shout and then a step.
Guess Who stood beside the ghoul
Who stirred the stinky mess?

"I'll take that." The Lord now spoke
As night turned into day.
"Well, Sir, you see, I kept them warm
Until You came this way.
The little dears had become lost,
And then they just dropped in.
I just happened to have this pool
Where they could take a swim!"

One look from Him, and Devil shrank
and crawled into his cave.
A slotted spoon in His right hand
Fished out the sweating babes.
"Too near to cooking in the pot,
You all had come to be.
Take my advice to live your life
With a look before you leap!"

The (Endless) Conversation

David Story

Pray without ceasing.
1 Thessalonians 5:17 (KJV)

Nicholas awoke to the ringing from the bell tower, signaling the call to morning prayer. He immediately, though slowly and with purpose, went to his knees. The springs on his cot made a creaking sound as his elbows rested on the thin mattress. The conversation began.

He walked from his sleeping quarters across the courtyard to the kitchen, where he would begin the preparations for the morning meal. The fog was still thick as Nicholas glided across the yard. His robe barely grazed the grass beneath his feet. His feet were bare and cold. His body shivered. And the conversation continued.

The small kitchen found light only by the sunrays that were just coming up above the horizon and making their way through the windows. Nicholas breathed a joyful sigh as he walked through one of the rays and made his way to the kitchen utensils hanging on hooks suspended from the low-rise ceiling. And the conversation heightened.

Soon, the preparation of the various foods was well under way, and the kitchen was alive with wonderful sounds. There was the clanging of pots and pans, and words were passed as each worker did their part to make sure the meal was ready on time. Nicholas continued with his work. And the conversation grew.

The meal ready, Nicholas and the rest of the kitchen workers began to serve. Each would take a portion of the food out to the long wooden tables in the dining area, where the brothers were seated, ready for the partaking of bread.

Bowls were passed from person to person, as each tore a piece of bread from the loaves provided. When everyone had a piece of bread in hand, one man stood and began to speak. And the conversation became one of thanks.

The meal over and the kitchen once again clean and ready for the preparation of meals to come, Nicholas made the trek back to his quarters. As he walked, he enjoyed the morning sun and felt the warmth on his face and shoulders. Mountaintops peered above the halls of the great monastery. And the conversation became one of amazement and awe.

Back at his quarters, he once again fell to his knees and assumed the position that had begun his day. All sound was blocked out as he became one with his Maker.

The unending prayer continued.

And it was a prayer of love, gratitude, humility . . . and peace.

"The time of business does not with me differ from the time of prayer; and in the noise and clutter of my kitchen, while several persons are at the same time calling for different things, I possess God in as great tranquility as if I were upon my knees at the Blessed Sacrament."

~ Brother Lawrence (*The Practice Of the Presence of God*)

$\mathcal{A}$ $\mathcal{L}$ove $\mathcal{U}$nending

MARILEE WILLIAMS ALVEY

$\mathcal{J}$IM BROKE TWO EGGS into the skillet, then punctured the yolks with a fork. He smiled as he stirred.

". . . and the two shall become one."

The intended recipient of the bounty sat silently, a plastic bib snapped around her neck.

"Holly, it's Christmas morning. Remember our traditional breakfast when the kids were young?" He paused. "Breakfast pizza and gooey rolls. I remember you used to stay up until all hours putting that casserole together on Christmas Eve."

He pushed the eggs around slowly with the spatula. Scooping them up on a plate, he carried them proudly to where she sat. Lifting a spoonful to her mouth and pressing it gently against her bottom lip, he lovingly placed the contents into her slightly open mouth.

"Remember the stockings? You picked out treasures perfectly suited to each child. Remember that toy hamster you found that danced and sang to a breakdance song? It was Ben's. Right?"

He searched into her blue-grey eyes for some spark, but she'd moved out many years ago. Fifteen years had passed since Alzheimer's ripped into her. At first, she'd only misplaced things, then she misplaced herself. Finally, she'd misplaced her family.

Jim wasn't complaining, for it was through having to take her place that he could truly appreciate all the love she had given. She had fed him, now he would feed her, pure and simple. As he lifted another spoonful to her lips, he thought about her sacrifice. Never earning any money of her own; laying aside her own dreams to make a loving home.

He had risen to the top of his occupation as an international airline captain only by her taking his place. While he traveled the world, she wiped up vomit and changed sheets. She attended the ball games, the school conferences, and the high school performances. She had been the wind beneath his wings. So when she became frightened when he wasn't nearby, he clipped his wings and never looked back.

Tenderly he wiped the remnants of egg from her mouth, then pushed her wheelchair into the bedroom. "The kids will be coming in two hours. Time to decorate my Christmas tree."

He lovingly removed her nightgown and placed a towel over her to chase away the chill as he began her sponge bath.

Going to the closet, he took out a festive Christmas sweater. A lap robe would, of necessity, finish the ensemble.

He brushed her greying hair and added a Christmas bow to keep it from falling in her eyes.

Jim stood back and gazed at her with admiration. She was his shining star.

Long ago, he used to tease her, saying that if he died before her, he'd take a lawn chair outside Heaven and wait until she arrived. He was certain that if he waited, he would eventually live in her mansion (instead of the shack he would, no doubt, have earned). He now realized that she had given him one more gift: growth through sacrificial service to her. Jim felt certain that he, too, would now feel at home in Heaven.

Secretly, Jim felt that Holly would not leave him until he'd filled up the basket of love she had emptied in service to him and the kids. It was a bushel basket, and he'd started well behind.

He smiled as the kids arrived, each kissing her on the cheek and hugging her. She was a gift that had been opened and emptied for them, and they knew it instinctively.

Christmas was always Holly's favorite holiday, the time when her gifts of cooking, service and hospitality magically came together. And so it seemed only fitting that she left him on that very night.

"The first face she'll recognize in eight long years will be that of Jesus," he mused as everyone sang *Silent Night*.

He wiped away some tears. No one thought it out of place. He'd known she was gone a half hour before. Her head bowed as if she'd fallen asleep, but they'd become so close that Jim could feel her love leave the room, like a sigh.

Later, he would tell the kids she had died in her sleep, as, indeed, she did.

Alone now, he walked behind her wheelchair, gently wrapping his arms around his wife one more time. He softly kissed her hair. "I love you with a love unending," he whispered, to Holly . . . and her Maker.

Too Much Salt in the Cookies

STEPHANIE BULLARD

THE COOKIES HAD TOO much salt.

Watching her two-year-old granddaughter push a chair over to the counter and climb onto it like it was a mountain to be scaled, the grandmother's eyes filled with drops of salty moisture.

When the little girl turned with a triumphant smile and said, "Me wanna help too, Gan-ma," the drops eased over the edges of her eyes and slid in easy tracks down her cheeks.

Before she could wipe them away, they slipped off her cheeks and splattered their saltiness into the dough.

Too much salt.

But as the grandmother and granddaughter shared a cookie later, she thought they tasted like sweetness itself.

The cookies had too much salt.

Watching her eight-year-old granddaughter tie an old, checked apron with fastidious and serious precision, the grandmother's eyes filled with drops of salty moisture.

When the child turned to offer a gap-toothed grin and said, "Let's make them extra-chocolaty this time, Grandma," the drops spilled over the edges of her eyes and sped in tiny ribbons down her cheeks.

She didn't bother to wipe them away, so they dripped off her cheeks and plopped their saltiness into the dough.

Too much salt.

But as grandmother and granddaughter shared the cookies later, with plenty of milk and giggles, she thought they tasted like happiness itself.

The cookies had too much salt.

Watching her fifteen-year-old granddaughter jerk on her coat and grab the car keys, the grandmother's eyes filled with drops of salty moisture.

When the teen turned with an impatient scowl and said, "I just don't have time to bake stupid cookies. I have better things to do," the drops flowed over the edges of her eyes and tracked down her cheeks in sorrowful streaks.

She wiped at them, but there were too many, and as she bowed her head, they slipped off her cheeks and buried their saltiness into the dough.

Too much salt.

Later, as the grandmother ate a cookie by herself, she thought it tasted like disappointment itself.

The cookies had too much salt.

Watching her grandmother explain the process of cookie-making to the infant she held, the twenty-three-year-old granddaughter's eyes filled with drops of salty moisture.

When the grandmother turned with a withered smile and said, "This was always my favorite thing to do with you," the drops seeped over the edges of her eyes and slid down her cheeks in happy rivulets.

Her hands full of baby, she couldn't wipe them away, and they slipped off her cheeks and splashed their saltiness into the dough.

Too much salt.

But as granddaughter and grandmother shared a cookie later, she thought they tasted of memories themselves.

The cookies had too much salt.

Watching a replay of a hundred memories in her mind, the granddaughter's eyes filled with drops of salty moisture. As she pictured her grandmother's smile and whispered words, *"I'll always love you,"* the drops gushed over the edges of her eyes and rushed down her cheeks in pain-filled rivers.

Placing both hands on the counter, she dropped her head and let the tears streak off her cheeks and spread their saltiness into the dough.

Too much salt.

As the granddaughter laid a cookie on her grandmother's grave, the taste of bittersweet memories filled her heart until it overflowed.

Divinity Pie

KENN ALLAN

INGREDIENTS:

⅓ dry measure clay/dust, freshly ground
⅔ cup lukewarm water
1 pinch salt (of the earth)
1 essence of soul
1 pkg. activated yeast
2 tablets moral fiber
Manna, white
Milk and honey
1 vial oil
1 loaf of bread, broken
1 cup red wine
1 Holy Spirit (no substitutes)
Assorted fresh fruit (love, faith, humility, etc.)
Blessings
Garnish (optional)

DIRECTIONS:

Combine clay (or dust), water, and salt in a medium-sized creation.

Place soul into the palm of one hand and blow it gently into the mixture.

Add activated yeast. Stir freely until all ingredients are well-blended.

Cover with blessing and set aside to spontaneously ferment.

Preheat oven to highest temperature (Fervent).

When mixture reaches an internal temperature of 98.6°F (37°C), insert moral fiber tablets; take special care not to break.

Pour entire mixture into a (gold) non-stick crucible and form a vessel by pressing mixture firmly against bottom and sides.

Sprinkle with manna as needed, to maintain desired consistency.

NOTE: Mixture may stiffen if left unattended. Remove any hardened portions and discard immediately.

In ancient receptacle, mix equal amounts of milk and honey; simmer over low heat until thickened. Carefully pour liquid into crucible until all is fulfilled. Separation is common at this stage of preparation; adding a few drops of oil will encourage cohesiveness (multiple anointings may be necessary).

Cover crucible with a protective lid and place into preheated oven. Actual baking time may vary; allow extended patience for those living at lower elevations.

At the appointed hour, break bread into single servings and mix with cup of red wine.

Remove crucible from oven as quickly as possible; it is very hot and will inflict severe wounds to the palms of both hands. Pour the bread/wine mélange freely into crucible. Cover and set aside for three days until risen.

Remove lid for the last time. This will cause crucible to crack down the middle and fall away. Use a wooden cross to skim away any/all sins which have bubbled to the surface; discard.

While still warm, saturate the entire new creation with the Holy Spirit, insuring abundant flow into the crust's deepest cracks and crevices.

Arrange fresh fruit (not canned) on all surface areas in a unique and wonderful design. Season with blessings (to taste) and garnish with a sprig of personality.

SERVES: 1

 A Grain of Faith

MID STUTSMAN

~⚹~

HE SLOW, STEADY PLODDING of Clancy, a Belgian draft horse, was the only sound to break the silence of a cold January morning in Indiana. The year was 1853, and the winter was a hard one, with snow accumulations nearing four feet. The temperatures held steady at zero, but the frigid wind pulled them down into the minus twenties.

Bundled against the biting cold, John Yoder sat astride his faithful horse. Saddle bags held steaming loaves of fresh baked bread, doomed to be frozen by the time they were delivered.

John tried not to fret. "At least they'll stay fresher longer."

He shivered, in spite of wearing several woolen layers and having hot baked potatoes stuffed into his pockets. Coming out on this frigid day was not something he had looked forward to, but it was a most urgent act of mercy. He had been informed the day before about a young family in desperate need of help. A traveling cobbler had stumbled upon them by accident.

"Name's Loucks. Only spoke to the missus—Emily," said the cobbler. "Don't know much about 'em, 'cept there's young 'uns. I would have stayed to help out, but I have three families still waitin' to have their yearly shoes made."

It didn't take long for John to recognize the prodding of the Holy Spirit, and he set about his task without question. The trip was slow and arduous, giving him time to think about his life. He'd traveled to Indiana from the Ohio valley with expectations of establishing a bakery in the quaint little town of Wabash. Daily he prayed for a wife who would love to bake alongside him.

On arrival, his hopes were dashed upon finding a bakery already opened. Yet, in spite of the discouraging setback and lack of unmarried women, his faith remained strong.

He staked a claim on twenty acres of land near the town, built his house, and planted wheat. For the time being, he decided, he could at least perfect his trade.

He carved the words "I am the Bread of Life" into the oak beam over his hearth, and while he waited to see his dreams realized, he baked. No visitor went away without a fragrant loaf to sample. He had faith that word would spread and he would soon be open for business.

A low whicker from Clancy drew John away from his thoughts. He turned to check the sled pulling sacks of wheat and provisions for the struggling family. It all looked intact beneath the roped canvas cover.

Satisfied, he patted the horse and looked up to see the humble cabin nestled in a forest of maple trees and red-twig dogwoods, but the lack of smoke coming from the chimney chased the smile from his face. Fearful, John urged Clancy forward.

"Dear Father, please . . ." he prayed, as he moved snow away from the unlatched door. In the dim light of the single room, he saw only a mound of blankets and furs piled in front of a cold fireplace. He shook them, but there was no evidence of life.

"Mr. Loucks? Mrs. Loucks?" he whispered, unwilling to believe God had taken him there for naught. He lifted a corner of the covers and stared at a pale woman, who struggled to open her eyes. Her chapped lips quivered when she spoke. "I tr-tried to keep the f-fire going."

John ran to get kindling and some small logs, and began setting a fire. When the flames took, he grabbed a bowl and filled it with clean snow to melt. After offering water to the mother, he hurried to get more wood, while she nursed her twin baby boys. Mr. Loucks, he learned, had been killed in a logging accident.

Once the fire was roaring, Emily pulled back the covers and sat with her arms wrapped around her sons. In spite of what she had gone through, she looked lovely, and John wondered at the stirring he felt in his heart. He retrieved his saddlebags and knelt before her.

"Mrs Loucks. I mean, Emily. Do you . . . what I mean is . . . well, you shouldn't eat this too fast," he blurted out.

Emily saw the bread and wept. "Thank you. For everything."

Their hands touched as she brought the loaf close to her face. She drew in a deep breath, and then murmured softly, "I love to bake bread."

PART TWO

Art Attack

The Garish Orange Frame

Debbie Roome

*T*T WAS SUITABLE PUNISHMENT, I suppose. Fifty hours of community service in payment for one act of vandalism. I'd thought it funny at the time—letting the air out of the wheelchair's tires—but looking back, it was pretty dumb.

My heart plummeted when I heard where my sentence was to be served. The Haven. A home for those with physical and intellectual disabilities. Around town, it was commonly called the "funny farm."

It was the last place a cool teenager wanted to be. My friends cackled like hyenas when they found out.

I noticed the picture frame the very first day the social worker marched me through the doors. It was hard to miss as it was almost as tall as I, and it was so bright. The garish orange plaster had to be four inches wide and it was pocked with bits of broken mirror and lime green beads. Some clown had daubed purple paint here and there, and the whole effect was seriously ugly. It dominated an entire wall in the reception area.

I initially worked at the home for three hours each weekend, and the frame was the first thing I saw each time I dragged myself through the doors. *Ugly*, I thought. Ugly like the judge who had sent me here.

I wasn't a willing worker, but the staff was glad of my assistance anyway, and soon trained me in the basics of caregiving. It was an uncomfortable process: learning to change nappies on a teenager, spoon-feeding those with limited movement, wiping drool from a ten-year-old's chin, reading *Chicken Little* to an eighteen-year-old.

My social life suffered and soon I was alone on the weekends.

"Funny farmer," my friends would chant. "Shelley belongs on the funny farm."

One day I realized they weren't the type of friends I wanted and turned my attention to completing my community service so I could move on with life.

I doubled my hours at The Haven, and before I knew it, the kids started to worm their way into my heart. Henry was a giant eight-year-old with bug eyes and a terrible stutter. He spent his days crawling around the playroom, and whenever he saw me arrive he would shout, "M-m-me first. Shelly h-h-help me f-f-first."

Then there was Martin. He would face the corner and rock on his knees, murmuring to himself. One day I went and rocked with him, and later he calmly allowed me to feed him. Great progress, according to the staff.

My favorite, however, had to be Alyssa. She was sixteen and had been born with no legs, stumps for arms, and severe mental impairment. Nevertheless, her eyes shone whenever she saw me. I would sit with her, rubbing cream into her withered stumps and singing softly so only she could hear. She reminded me of an angel, with her short blonde curls and clear, babyish skin.

It was at the start of my ninth shift that I finally noticed the painting inside the garish orange frame. Of course, it had always been there, but the frame had drawn my attention away from the true artwork.

The delicate watercolor depicted a golden-haired toddler in a wheelchair, sitting in a garden of beautiful roses and fountains. A soft pink blanket was wrapped around her torso, and where her hands should have been were shrunken stumps. A small sign rested on her lap and I moved closer to read the neat, fluid script.

> *At last you've noticed me,*
> *Seen past the frame that holds me in . . .*
> *Don't be put off by my body, my exterior*
> *Look past that and see the real me*
> *I feel pain as you do*
> *I feel rejection as you do*
> *I rejoice at the wind in my hair*
> *And love a beautiful garden as you do*
> *Will you look past the frame . . .*
> *And see who I really am?*

I stood there for at least ten minutes, tears running down my cheeks. Eventually, the receptionist came and pressed a tissue into my hand.

I nodded to the child. "Alyssa?"

She nodded. "Her father painted that and presented it to the home when she moved in." She smiled gently. "It always has an impact when people truly see it."

The Gallery

Kenn Allan

I am a wanderer by choice—
A life in which I oft rejoice;
I pay no heed to any voice
Except my very own.
Through villages and glades I roam
With no desire to claim a home
Or share my name by tongue or tome
Lest sins I must atone.

I walk this life alone . . .

Upon this day uniquely blessed,
When men of faith aspire to rest,
I set upon an anxious quest
To flee a vengeful storm;
But as I stagger up the street,
Damp cobblestones beneath my feet,
I find doors bolted in defeat
To thwart my freezing form.

I shiver to get warm . . .

But what is this to catch my eye
Between the earth and angry sky—
A door ajar which dares defy
The fury of the gale?
Persuaded by a lightning flash,
Across the sodden street I splash

And o'er the threshold boldly crash
In effort to prevail.

Death waits if I should fail . . .

A silver bell above the door
Rings with a voice I've heard before
While I stand dripping on the floor
Inside the tiny room;
No living soul is glimpsed at all
Or harkens my expectant call;
I have no hint what might befall
Or lurk beyond the gloom.

Dead silence, like a tomb . . .

As I squint, perceptions shifting,
Watching shrouds of darkness lifting,
My attention keeps on drifting
Toward a shadowed nook—
On six easels, neatly covered,
Six large paintings gently hovered;
Works of art yet undiscovered
Or, perhaps, forsook.

I must go have a look . . .

Unveiled, the first is rather trite—
A study sketched in black and white
Which shows how dark defines the light
Like night contrasts the day;
As observation lingers on
My first impressions are foregone;
I sense my passions strangely drawn
To interim shades of gray.

I shrug and turn away . . .

The next is hard to ascertain—
It's not unlike a water stain
As if once used to capture rain
Or trap the morning dew.
I risk a touch; the pigment smears
And trickles down like human tears,
Drips to the floor, then disappears
Beyond my narrow view.

I search my heart anew . . .

The third work I can understand—
A painting filled with sea and land,
Created by a skillful hand
And brushed with classic style.
Within a maple's spreading lace
I almost see the artist's face
While every leaf he dabs in place
With a delighted smile.

I marvel for a while . . .

The fourth in line is quite bizarre—
The sun, the moon, one blazing star
Perform a concert from afar
Against a velvet sky;
In perfect harmony they sing
While eons form an endless ring
And autumn dances with the spring
Before their time is nigh.

I take a breath, and sigh . . .

A touch of whimsy marks the fifth,
Which tells a most amusing myth,
Where fishes ferry birds forthwith
Between two distant shores;

On finny friends, the birds recline
As if intended by design,
Propelled across the surging brine
By love instead of oars.

My yearn for friendship soars . . .

Still pondering five paintings past,
I stand before the sixth and last
And pray the artist had surpassed
The rest by some degree;
But as I pull the velvet drape,
I stagger back, my mouth agape—
The face portrayed cannot escape
Familiarity . . .

The portrait is of me!

But unlike those I viewed before,
This painting needs of something more—
The lack of detail and decor
Leaps from the gilded frame;
Even so, it looms commanding,
Incompleteness notwithstanding;
I am lost, my brain demanding
Cause for such acclaim.

What is this artist's name?

I scan the canvas for a clue
To whom my gratitude is due
So I might ask him why he drew
My sketch in such a rush;
There in one corner, something odd
Tucked just above the gilt facade—
The artist signed my portrait ~GOD~
And left behind His brush.

I cannot help but blush . . .

Daylight comes, the storm abated,
Adding warmth to art created;
I can see, although belated,
Through eyes which understand;
Now I'll wander roads uncharted
With the paintbrush He imparted
Adding to the work He started
Just the way He planned . . .

I'll trace the Artist's hand.

The Stand-In

HELEN PAYNTER

'ADN'T THE FOGGIEST IT would be so boring. The brocade round me neck is itching summ'at awful. I dare'nt move me 'and, so I wriggle me shoulders until 'e barks, "Stand still."

So I do, tryin' to think of summ'at else to take me mind off it.

The dress is killing me under me shoulders. I'm a bit plumper than 'er, I s'pose. I wonder if 'e'll paint in the little creases where the fabric is stretched across me bust.

The job sounded so fancy when 'e first showed up. Mind you, I was up to me eyes in fish scales at the time, so I weren't feeling picky.

"Excuse me, miss."

Ever so polite 'e was. A real gentleman, me ma said, when I took him to meet 'er later.

"Excuse me, miss. I wonder if you'd be interested in being a model for me? I paint portraits, you see."

Well, my William looked 'bout ready to fillet 'im like a mackerel as 'e stood there, 'is 'at in 'is 'and like a proper toff. 'E obviously realized 'e'd started off badly, so 'e quickly explained. *"Nothing improper, I promise you. You could bring a chaperone, of course. You see, I've been commissioned to paint the Duchess of Barnstable's eldest daughter. A coming-out portrait. She's a famous beauty, but the thing is, she can only let me have three sittings, so I need a stand-in. Someone who resembles her. To wear her dress. Stand in her pose. And I saw you, and you're perfect."*

Well, I didn't need no second invite. I took off me apron and 'anded it to William, 'oo was scowling fit to bust. And that's 'ow I ended up 'ere, me 'air piled on me 'ead like a Sunday pudding.

Now I've got cramp in me leg. I wonder if 'e'll notice if I bend it under me skirts . . .

Ow, ow. Oh no, there's the plinth gone. Mind you, it weren't good craftsmanship. Me dad could've done a better job with one 'and be'ind 'is back.

Oh, when's me hour up? It ain't no fun bein' a stand-in.

~⚬✸⚬~

We're 'avin' a break, and now 'e wants to talk. Showin' me 'is paintin's. Wants to show off, I s'pose.

"This is the Earl of Caernarvon."

"Well, 'e looks like he fancies 'imself, standing with 'is 'ands in 'is pockets like that."

"Yes, perhaps. It was remarkably difficult to persuade him that his pet pig didn't belong in the painting. He needed some mollifying after that, I seem to recall . . . Ah, yes, this is the Countess of Middlesex."

"And she's no better than she oughta be. Look at that dress. A wonder she didn't catch 'er death of cold. Catch me wearin' summat like that."

"Well, I couldn't possibly comment on that. But tell me, what sort of art do you like?"

"Art? Me? I never 'ave time for things like that. I've got me job at the fish stall, and then me ma and dad to cook for when I get 'ome. Us workin' folks ain't got time for yer fancy stuff."

"Well, I think that's a pity. Art can teach us so much. Now tell me, what do you think of this?"

'E pulls out an enormous painting. Dark, it is. I can 'ardly make it out. Then I realize; it's a man on a cross. 'Alf a dozen women standin' around wringing their 'ands. Gloomy, I call it. Not what I'd want on me wall at 'ome.

Still, it's good to be polite. "Very nice. Sort of meaningful, I 'spect."

He looks at me with 'is 'ead on one side, like 'e's about to pick up 'is paintbrush. "Well, I like to think so. Do you know who it is?"

"What kind'a fool d'you take me for? Course I know 'oo it is."

"And do you know why he's doing it?"

"I ain't no university professor, mister. Ask them as knows."

"The thing is, it's not university professors who understand this best. It's ordinary people, like you and me."

"Well, speak for yerself, mister. I don't know nothin' about that."

"But you do; of course you do. You see, he was a stand-in, too."

"A stand-in? 'Oo for?"

"For you, Hettie. For me. You see, it's not just the toffs who need a substitute."

Unchained

TERI WILSON

PALOMA SWATTED THE FLY from her face and glopped more acrylic onto her canvas. Her easel wobbled in the mud. She was in the back corner of a swine barn, and although the swine themselves were absent, certain traces of them remained. One of which was their pungent aroma. Paloma tried to breathe without using her nostrils and returned to the task at hand.

Her subject was quivering on a grooming table, also standing in the mud.

Paloma made a comfortable living as a pet portrait artist. More often than not, she worked at dog shows where she quickly painted in broad strokes until the dogs were whisked away by their handlers to prance around the show ring.

For all the pomp and circumstance dog shows are afforded on television, they are remarkably unglamorous in real life. And smelly. Take today, for instance, with the dog show in a rodeo arena and the grooming area in the swine barn.

"Thank you so much! It's stunning!" the owner of the quivering Maltese on the table gushed.

"I'm glad you like it. Tell your friends I'll be here tomorrow, too."

"Oh, I will. I'm going to be back with a crowd of people around your easel."

The woman headed for the ring, and Paloma had a feeling she would be painting more than a few tiny white dogs tomorrow.

It was freezing in the barn and Paloma's teeth chattered while she packed up her supplies.

She was carefully maneuvering her van down a small stretch of Farm Road 316 when she saw him. Alone in the yard. He was shivering in the sleet, his head hanging down. His eyes squinted and he winced as icy drops pelted his face. Paloma had never seen anything so pitiful. Or cruel.

She pulled over and knocked on the door of the house. A burly man answered, clearly surprised to see a strange woman on his porch.

Paloma's confidence wavered, but she couldn't bring herself to walk away. "Um, sir, your dog is chained out in your yard and it's below freezing. Maybe he could come inside."

"Lady, he ain't allowed in the house."

"But he's shivering. Maybe you could put him in the garage or something?"

"He's an animal. He belongs outside."

Then Paloma found herself looking at the door, which had been slammed in her face. Defeated, she slumped back to her car and drove home in the slush.

All night, she was tortured by dreams of the heartbreaking black mutt cowering in the cold. First thing in the morning, she called Animal Care Services.

"We can't help you, ma'am."

"What do you mean? The poor dog is chained in the yard. Have you looked outside?" A blanket of sparkling snow covered the ground.

"It's perfectly legal to chain a dog, so long as it has food and water."

Later, back at the dog show, her eyes flashed with anger as she thought about the conversation. Another fluffy white dog sat before her, waiting to be immortalized on canvas. If she weren't so upset, she would have laughed at the irony of her situation. She was being paid thousands of dollars to paint a parade of spoiled dogs, and less than two miles away, a forgotten black mutt huddled alone in the frosty wind.

It was ridiculous, really. In art school, her professors had always talked about how great art could change the world. Yet she stood in a swine barn, painting the same white dog, over and over again.

"I'm sorry. I can't do this." Paloma dropped her slender paintbrush and frantically began packing. She shoved a fistful of dollars at the stunned dog owner with the Maltese and tromped back to her van in the snowy parking lot.

The black dog was still in the yard when the van slid to a halt. His muzzle was covered with a layer of snow flurries and his chain had hardened with ice.

Paloma saw the dog's owner watching her from inside the house as she unpacked the van on the side of the road. Her gloved fingers shook; she wasn't sure if it was the cold or fear. *Just let him come out here*, she thought. *He can't do anything to me. I'm not on his property and I'm not breaking any laws.*

Paloma secured her easel in the snow and set to work mixing the pigments on her palette. Then she began painting a picture which could change the world. At least, maybe, for one dog who lived on a chain.

A Peddler's Portrait

Betty Castleberry

The colorful old truck clattered down the street, attracting attention from a handful of people. It came to a stop on the courthouse square, and a rotund little man appeared from the cab. He squinted into the sun, then peered at the small crowd gathering around him. "Well, well. Good day, ladies and gentlemen." He rubbed his hands together and smiled, revealing a row of tiny, perfect teeth. "Albert Simmons at your service. May I show you some of my wares?"

Before anyone could reply, he opened a battered trunk and then pointed at a little boy who was staring intently at him. "Young man, I bet you would love to have this, wouldn't you?" One stubby hand held up a shiny silver cap gun.

The little boy's eyes twinkled, and he turned to a woman standing beside him. "Can I have it, Mom?"

She glanced at her son, then leveled her eyes at the peddler. "Mr. Simmons, I'm hesitant to let my child play with a gun. Even a cap gun."

"Oh, I quite understand, ma'am, but this isn't just an ordinary cap gun. Why no, it's a fine scale replica of the gun used by Doc Holliday in the shootout at the OK Corral. It'd be a treasure for any young man to have."

The little boy pulled on his mother's hand. "Please, Mom. I won't shoot it. I promise."

"I don't know." She faced Mr. Simmons again. "How much?"

"Nine dollars, ma'am, and you won't be sorry."

"I'll give you five."

"Done." He handed the gun to the boy. "Congratulations, young man."

Mr. Simmons turned his attention to a middle-aged woman. "For you, ma'am, I have something no kitchen is complete without." He took a box from the trunk. "This will chop, shred, or dice any fruit or vegetable in an instant. Surely you could use one of these."

"Well, I don't know. I ordered something like that from a TV ad once. It didn't really work very well."

"Oh, of course it didn't. You see this?" He pointed to the underside of the contraption. "The model I carry is the only one with this double-edged, surgical grade, stainless steel cutting blade. It's guaranteed. Surely you could use a wonderful time saver like this."

"Well, maybe. How much is it?"

"I can let you have this today for the special price of fourteen dollars."

"That sounds high. I wouldn't be interested."

"How about twelve dollars, and I'll throw in the mini chopper for free. I'd hate to see you pass up a bargain like this."

The woman rummaged through her purse. "I only have eleven dollars and thirty-seven cents."

"Close enough. Enjoy it, ma'am."

The little man paced for a moment, then zeroed in on an elderly gentleman.

"Sir, I've got just the thing for you. Do you ever have trouble sleeping?" He didn't wait for an answer. "Of course you do. We all do at times." He held up an oddly-shaped pillow. "If you had this, you'd sleep like a baby. Yes sir, this one hundred percent Fantastic Foam pillow molds to the curves of your neck and upper back, allowing for a perfect fit to your body's specific contours. I've got one myself. Can't sleep without it anymore."

Just as the elderly man was about to reply, a police officer walked up to the truck. "May I see your peddler's license?"

"Peddler's license? Why sir, I beg your pardon. I am not a peddler. No, not at all. I am an artist."

"An artist? I don't see any paintings."

"No sir, you don't. That's because I'm not that kind of an artist. I'm an expert in the art of salesmanship. Just like painters and sculptors create beautiful pieces of art, I create desire in people for things before they even realize they want them."

"You're a peddler without a license. I'll need to see your ID."

The little man frowned and handed his ID to the officer.

"I recognize this name. You've been arrested for this before."

The peddler looked at the handcuffs in the policeman's hand. "Surely we can overlook this little indiscretion just this once. I'll pack up and move along."

"Sorry. Hands behind your back."

"You don't have to use those, do you?"

The officer snapped the cuffs firmly around Mr. Simmons wrists. "Afraid I do, Michelangelo. I'm an artist, too, and these assist me in the art of persuasion."

Ceil's Egg Money

LAURIE GLASS

A purty gal, jes' like her ma,
Yep, that's my daughter, Ceil.
So proud that I could almost bust—
Well, that's jes' how I feel.

The missus died when Ceil was young,
I raised her on my own.
Not many girls around these parts,
Spent lots o' time alone.

And yet that girl seemed not t' mind,
Drew pictures in the dirt,
Whatever scene that she could find
But still kept up her work.

She asked for paper, pencil, too—
I pondered for a day.
Seemed silly, but she worked so hard,
So what else could I say?

Girl never griped, but aimed t' please,
And always did her chores.
Made up my mind t' tell her that
Egg money would be hers.

Ceil smiled big and squeezed me tight,
Then ran right out the door,
Collected eggs and got 'em washed
T' take 'em to the store.

She saved them pennies, all of 'em
Until she had enough
T' buy some paper, pencils, too—
Supplies for drawin' stuff.

Decided, too, that she should paint,
An' so she saved some more.
She ordered all that she would need
At that there gen'ral store.

The first thing that she painted—my!
She worked all day 'til night.
First glance, and I could see it looked
Like that ol' barn, a'right.

I saw how happy thet she was,
Good paintin' she could do,
An' always tol' her she did good,
An' raised more chickens, too.

Amazed at what thet girl could paint—
My purty daughter, Ceil.
It wasn't jes' what I could see,
Her pictures made me feel.

She saved egg money when she could,
A little at a time,
T' get some learnin' 'bout this art—
It's all that filled her mind.

I wanted her to stay, o' course,
But knew it couldn't be.
The day came she was all growed up,
An' said goodbye t' me.

She didn't know I cried sometimes
On my ol' lonely farm,
But smiled when I looked up et
That there paintin' o' the barn.

Ceil got her schoolin' sure enough,
Egg money put her through.
I sent it to her all the time
T' make her dreams come true.

She took t' sellin' off her art—
The money she has made!
Stopped needin' that egg money sent,
Her way was always paid.

Egg money sat up in a jar
An' things jes' weren't the same,
I took a mind t' visit her—
Used money for the train.

Got neighbor boy t' do the chores
An' packed m' Sunday clothes,
An' took an extra bath an' all
To see them city folks.

So here I am and I can see
My Ceil and all her art,
She's happy an' she's done so good—
Lifts up this feller's heart.

A purty gal, jes' like her ma,
Yep, that's my daughter, Ceil.
So proud that I could almost bust—
Well, that's jes' how I feel.

Kevin Byrd's Secret

Erin Brannan

H E WAS THE QUIETEST one in the class, and he sat two seats in front of me, his head perpetually bent over his desk. It took me a few days to figure out what he was doing.

Each day, as soon as Miss Fleck dimmed the lights and flipped on the overhead projector, he pulled out a thick pad of paper and a pencil and hunched over it secretively. From the way his wrist moved, I could tell he wasn't taking notes. He was drawing.

He was new to my high school. His name was Kevin Byrd, but through the cruelty of teenagers he had become Kevin Nerd, or Byrd the Nerd. His constant drawing didn't help matters.

One day, out in the quad, I watched from my picnic table as Bo Simpson and his clan came up behind Kevin and smacked his pad of paper to the ground. Kevin's eyes went wide with panic as Bo swiftly picked it up and dangled it in his face.

Please . . . don't open it, I prayed silently, feeling Kevin's embarrassment.

Bo threw the book back on the ground, making Kevin stoop down in the muddy grass to pick it up.

I turned away before I started to cry.

I didn't know Kevin at all, but then he didn't seem to know anyone at all.

He wasn't stupid; I could tell by the little half smile that danced across his lips after Miss Fleck handed back our trig tests. He wasn't ugly, either. With a haircut, he'd actually be better-looking than Bo. But he was awkward and antisocial, and in high school it took a lot less than that to be exiled.

Sometimes I thought about coming up alongside him after class and saying, "Hi, I'm Lanie," or "You draw, too?" but everything sounded so stupid in my head.

One day, Jenny Simon (who sits in front of me) was sick, and Kevin turned around to pass our worksheets back. I tried to smile at him, but he just grunted and whipped around in his seat.

It was a Tuesday when he finally spoke to me. Class was almost over when the fire alarm went off. The morning announcements hadn't mentioned a fire drill, so Miss Fleck took the alarm seriously. A few girls in the back of the room began to speak in hurried tones about the fire being real.

Just as we were all about to get up, Principal Michaels' voice came over the loudspeaker. "Teachers and students, this is not a drill. There is a fire in the cafeteria and we need everyone to evacuate immediately. Please remain calm and exit the building by your nearest fire exit."

The girls behind me were now hysterical, and one of them was crying. Suddenly, everyone began to rush to the front of the room. Miss Fleck was yelling for us to calm down, but the frenzied girls had gotten everyone riled up.

As I rose to exit, Jenny tripped on her backpack and fell on Kevin, knocking him to his knees. His pad, which had been clutched protectively against his chest, fell on the floor, spilling open. No one else noticed.

The girls behind me pushed past, stepping on the papers before running to the door. Kevin immediately bent down and began collecting his papers. I stooped to help him.

"You don't have to help me," he said without looking up.

I wasn't helping him, actually. I was on my knees, motionless, staring at the picture in my hand. It was a picture of me, and it was beautiful. The soft charcoal of the pencil created lines and shades that somehow made the pencil-drawn me look like a supermodel. I must've made a noise because Kevin looked up and his face turned scarlet.

Before he could speak, I whispered, "I can't believe this."

"I'm sorry," he stammered. "Please don't be mad. I draw everyone."

He held up the other sheets, and I saw Jenny, and Miss Fleck, and even Bo staring back at me.

Miss Fleck called back to us to hurry. Everyone else was heading out the door.

I smiled and looked Kevin right in the eye. "I'm not mad," I said. "These are amazing." I paused for a moment, studying the drawings. "They're all great, Kevin, but mine is . . . well it's different. It makes me look . . . beautiful."

Kevin cocked his head to the side and stood. "That's because you are." He grinned and headed toward the door.

An Artist—Sort of . . .

VERNA COLE MITCHELL

I could not paint a mountain view,
Not even if I wanted to . . .
But I can have within my goals
To bring God's peace to troubled souls.

I could not sculpt a bust of clay
If I took lessons every day . . .
But I can give a word of cheer
That someone badly needs to hear.

I could not sing an aria,
Nor could I lead an orchestra . . .
But I can help a fallen friend
To find his way back home again.

I could not dance in a ballet,
Nor kick my heels in any way . . .
But I can do a thoughtful deed
Or help someone who is in need.

I could not play a piano,
A tuba or a bass cello . . .
But I can always do my part
To show the world a caring heart.

Of all the arts there are to use,
The art of kindness will I choose.
I'll show His love in concrete ways
And pray my life to bring Him praise.

The Restoration

Larry Elliott

"CAN YOU DO ANYTHING?" Mary pleaded. "I know it's a mess, but this is my most prized possession and I—"

"Relax. Have a seat. Have a drink," the handsome young man interrupted, motioning to an elegant, well-stocked bar in a corner of the plush waiting area.

"No, thanks. I just need this repaired, quickly." Mary knew she appeared frantic.

He glanced at his Rolex before gently running his fingers across the canvas. A chill coursed her spine. "It is in pretty bad shape." He stated the obvious.

"I know that! What I want . . . *need* to know is if you can fix it?"

"Not to be . . . judgmental, but someone has already made a pathetic attempt to . . . 'touch up' this masterpiece. I must be honest, it is quite nearly ruined."

"I understand all that. I thought I could do it myself. I read books, watched videos, even took classes. But I've ruined it, haven't I?"

Tears were forthcoming.

Mary could sit no longer. She reached for her treasure and accidentally touched the man's hand. He jerked away, but not quick enough.

A bolt of lightning shot straight into her soul, and for an instant, the figure behind the counter resembled anything but a man. In fear, she grabbed her painting and ran, stumbling out the doorway and into a passerby.

Sprawled on the ground, just inches from the busy street, Mary noticed the stranger had managed to grab her painting from where it had fallen—rescuing it from certain destruction by the constant stream of traffic. Helping her to her feet, he offered her the artwork.

"I'm s-so s-sorry," Mary stuttered. "Are you okay?"

"I'm fine. And you? You look so unhappy."

"I . . ." Mary sobbed.

"There, now. Tell me your troubles. Among other things, I'm a good listener. Come, there's a cafe around this corner."

Curiously at ease, she followed his lead.

After unloading all her desperation, the stranger told her of just the place she sought.

"Will you take me there, now? You've done so much, and I hate to ask, but . . ."

"It's okay. I'll be happy to show you the way. It's not far. Follow me."

Once inside another waiting room, Mary noticed it was not as lavish, lacking the expensive niceties of the previous one. "Who is this master of restoration?" she asked.

"I am," the stranger answered.

Mary was taken aback, but only momentarily. "Can you fix the mess I've made of this? Please say you can."

Tenderly, he touched the canvas.

Haunted by her previous experience, Mary hesitantly touched his hand. Instead of a frightening specter, she beheld the man just as he was, only now surrounded by a golden aura.

"Yes, I can." He smiled. "Though the price may seem . . . unusual."

"Just tell me. I have fifty thousand dollars. You can take it all."

"No." He continued to smile. "Money cannot buy what I must do to restore this piece."

Puzzled, Mary begged for explanation.

"Treasures of this world are meaningless to me. If I am to perform a complete restoration on this piece, first you must grant me absolute ownership."

"What? Are you insane? I want it repaired so I can enjoy it. This is more precious than all of my other possessions together. Why would I just give it away?"

"That is the price, and I guarantee that no one else can do with this what I can. I will restore it wholly to its creative master's original condition."

Somehow, she knew he was telling the truth.

"Will I be able to come and look at it sometime?"

"You must trust me. You will be more than pleased when I am finished."

"How . . . long will it take?"

"Not as long as you might think."

"Okay, take it." She looked longingly at the framed catastrophe. "Before I change my mind."

The man set the painting on a stained wooden easel and produced a brush.

"You're going to do it here . . . now?"

"Why, yes."

"May I watch?"

"I insist."

In awe, Mary observed as he opened his palm and dipped the brush into a tiny pool of red. He lightly touched the center of the painting of Mary's ruined life and instantly restored it to its intended beauty.

Lesson One

LINDA WATSON OWEN

Once Lucifer, before the fall,
picked up his brush to paint.
"I think that I will really try
to make what is and ain't!"

So dip he did into his hues
of black and gray and white,
and with a giggle, gleefully
glopped everything in sight.

A swirling swish, a dribbly dab,
he didn't stop for luncheon.
He saw an angel passing by
and blurred him to a smudgeon.

"Just wait 'til God gets hold of you!"
the angel warned the imp,
"When He does, you bet it won't
be my wings that get clipped!"

"Oh, don't be such a fuddy-dud.
I'm just a havin' fun.
A slight redecoratin' never
has hurt anyone."

So off Luce went, with brush in hand,
to find another victim;
Michael came, and yep, you're right,
the little devil picked him.

"No, you don't!" Michael grabbed
to keep the imp from slingin'.
Sidestep saved the brush and pail,
but stumbling dipped a wing in.

A few quick flips and paint was flicked
all over pre-creation.
The rumble that ensued became
a heavenly sensation.

Cherubs gathered all around
to see the sloppy action
as Michael and that Lucifer
became the main attraction.

Paintball parties now can't hold
a candle to that chaos—
a swirling, twirling hurricane
of black 'n' white 'n' gray dots.

Then Gabriel yelled, "Cut it out!
You'll get us all in trouble!
Give me the paint; give me that brush,
now stop it on the double!"

Well, you can guess, he got his wish.
He got the paint and bucket,
but way too soon for him to see
he really should have ducked it.

So on it went, this paint melee,
the devil's glopping glory,
a churning mess, without a rest,
but there's more to this story.

You see, obedience is key
to God's high holy plan.
You'll find no beauty, find no art,
without the Great I Am.

God took the brush with just one word,
as all looked on in wonder,
amidst the imp's destructive spree
and selfish plunder blunders.

That brush in God's great mighty hand
soon shriveled into dust,
and all commotion that had been,
grew silent, mute, and hushed.

Holding breath, all bowed in awe,
with reverent fear and shudders,
and not one wing dared to arise
in halo-tickling flutters.

Silence reigned without a sound.
All braced for what was coming.
They waited—waited—waited more,
all heavenly pulses running.

Cautiously each eye was raised.
None dared know what to think.
Then suddenly God turned around
and gave them all a wink.

"You want to paint? Create some art?
I understand that passion.
Now take a lesson. Gather round,
and see what I will fashion."

A trembling from within the void
at once begins the story,
as rumbling through the mess they saw
a hint of coming glory.

God raised His arms and breathed upon
the face of darkened seas.
With a smile and one more wink,
He then said, "LET THERE BE!"

The words went forth in blooming hues,
a burst of dazzling light,
and all the angels sparkled, too,
as day broke through the night.

Heaven cheered to see the art
that poured from God's great hand.
Such vibrancy had ne'er been seen
since God's own time began.

God's laughter rang and life appeared
with fins, and feet, and paws,
as cherubs chattered with delight
and broke into applause.

Then one more time, a whispered hush
descended by God's hand,
as God Himself knelt in the earth
and formed His art named "man."

The eyes of Heaven looked upon
this masterpiece God formed
and watched in awe as His own breath
gave life to flesh new born.

But Lucifer, unlike the rest,
sneered at the reformed dirt,
and kicked at stardust in the sky's
dark corner where he lurked.

"Talk about art!" arch Michael said,
"Now that is how it's done!
Next time you feel like painting,
just remember Lesson One."

PART THREE

Lost in a Good Book

Iron and Ice

Jan Ackerson

I CLOSED THE FRONT DOOR behind me, knowing that Rick was on the other side, either weeping or praying. Unlike Rick, I had forgotten how to weep, and I had not prayed since the night God took Lissa from us. On that horrible night, I had cried out: *Why? You don't need Lissa in heaven, but I need her here!* Failing to change God's mind, I had turned my back on Him and barricaded my heart.

And now I was leaving—not because of anything Rick had done, but because the house was strangling me. Every room was thick with memories of my little girl. Lissa making a bubble bath beard. Lissa covered with cookie icing and colored sugar. Lissa sleeping, with a stuffed monkey tied to her wrist. Lissa playing right-hand melodies on the piano. She was alive everywhere, but I could not grasp her, and I felt myself turning to iron.

I promised Rick that I'd return, and fled to my parents' cabin on the lake, knowing that it would be chilly there in November. Cold hardens iron—I would embrace it. I had packed enough clothing for a week, maybe two, with no plans other than solitude and a respite from Rick's gentle pleading.

Come to church with me, Janey.

Let's go out, Janey.

Can we just talk for a while, Janey?

The first few days at the cabin passed in blessed numbness. I sat on the deck, wrapped in a blanket and staring at the lake, my thoughts dull and frosty. Waves tumbled to the beach and receded. Clouds drifted by, resembling nothing.

On the third day, however, an icy rain began before dawn and coated the deck with a crackling sheen. I sat on the worn sofa with a mug of coffee and listened to the minutes tick by, wishing that I had brought a book.

A desperate boredom led me to search the cabin for something to read. I had refused to bring a Bible, despite Rick's wordless gesture as I packed. *Don't you want to take this?* his eyes had said. But I was not speaking to its author, and I had no desire to read His book.

In a cupboard I remembered from childhood, I found several old board games, some plastic beach toys, a tattered collection of *Field and Stream* magazines, and a child's book of riddles. The magazines held no appeal for me—hundreds of indistinguishable pictures of deer, rifles, and fishermen in waders. Sighing deeply, I poured another cup of coffee and started to read the riddle book.

What did the duck say when she bought some lipstick?
~ Put it on my bill.

Have you heard about the new corduroy pillows?
~ They're making headlines.

What color is a cheerleader?
~ Yeller.

I choked on something unfamiliar—laughter. My face felt strange; I was using muscles that had been frozen for weeks. I closed my eyes and examined this emotion that threatened to feel like a betrayal of Lissa. All that came to me was an echo of her musical giggle. How she would have loved this book!

Where did Napoleon keep his armies?
~ In his sleevies.

What do you get when you cross a pond and a stream?
~ Wet feet.

How do you kill a circus?
~ Go for the juggler.

The tears that salted my lips were made of equal parts of grief and love, repentance and laughter. An iron door creaked open somewhere near my heart, and with each silly riddle, joy rushed in.

How exactly like God, I thought, to use this ridiculous book to thwart my stubborn spirit.

For two more days I stayed at the lake, while God transformed iron and ice into something warm and pliable; something human once more. Before I left,

I tore one riddle out of the book and tucked it into my pocket. It was one that would have tickled Lissa, and I wanted to tell it to Rick.

Why are pirates so popular?
~ *They just arrrrrr.*

I practiced my pirate voice all the way home.

Diversions

KENN ALLAN

I dread the autumn of my years
When summer dreams subside,
And balmy breezes haunt my room
By pushing drapes aside

To whisper nightmares in my ear
With warm and sultry breath—
Then drift away in light of day
Like harbingers of death.

It was upon a night like this
Not very long ago;
I stood in contemplation of
The courtyard far below.

My restless mind could not ignore
The passing of the breeze,
While dry leaves swirled, decayed and curled,
Amongst the dying trees.

I cast a prayer against the sky
Beseeching peaceful sleep,
It echoed back to reassure
My soul the Lord would keep;

And so I paced the weathered floor
Of my nocturnal plight—
The creaks and groans of age bemoans
The passing of the night.

"Enough!" I cried in fearful rage.
"Before all reason fades,
I must escape this wretched trap
From which sweet sleep evades."

So from my nightstand I retrieved
A heavy iron key
Kept in the drawer which fits a door
Few others ever see.

The mechanism of the lock
Protested my intrusions,
Then fell aside with rusty shrieks,
Removing all preclusions.

Holding high my bedside lamp,
I climbed the spiral stairs—
Though nearly blind, I vowed to find
Diversion from my cares.

The narrow steps abruptly end
Outside a rounded room
Where ideas flicker in delight
And wisdom cuts the gloom.

On sturdy shelves around the walls,
My cherished books were spread,
Crammed with notes and lifted quotes,
But mostly still unread.

My senses started spinning
From the churn of twisted plots,
The lure of musty leather,
And the tang of virgin thoughts.

I scanned the volumes carefully,
Deciding which to keep—
What might I find to fill my mind
And coax my soul to sleep?

I saw within my lofty reach
An abstruse book of verse,
Espousing deep philosophies
In which I could immerse.

As I reflect upon the mire,
My face is seldom shown—
These words impart the poet's heart
But speak not of my own.

Undaunted by my failed attempt,
I searched the shelves again
And found upon a gritty shelf
The crude affairs of men,

Where justice flew on angry fists
And sins repaid in kind—
A darker place, devoid of grace . . .
A world best left behind.

Perhaps a romance could entice
My passions to be stilled,
But found amongst the pages
Expectations unfulfilled;

Stories steeped in pleasure
And served up like hemlock tea—
My heart denies those lustful lies
Of love which cannot be.

I settled in to search all night
When something caught my eye—
A glint of gold beneath the dust
Of something shelved too high.

It was the Bible I once loved,
Neglected since my youth;
I dared to peek and thereby seek
God's everlasting truth.

I found His gentle wisdom
No mere human could contrive,
His righteous sense of justice
In which virtue can survive.

The love and peace the Lord bestows
On aging fools like me . . .
I searched no more, secured the door,
And threw away the key.

Line upon Line

ANN GROVER

"THIRTY-SEVEN . . . THIRTY-EIGHT . . . thirty-nine."

As Big Monty was released from the manacles, an unearthly moan seeped from his bloodied lips. He sprawled facedown, dust whirling around his oozing limbs and torso.

"Take him away."

Carefully, Bert and Dovie lifted Big Monty into the back of the wagon, mindful of the gaping slashes on his ebony back.

"You'll be fine, love," Dovie whispered in his ear.

Bert snapped the reins, and Monty groaned again as the wagon moved forward. Mercifully, the sounds ceased.

"He's out." Dovie stroked Monty's matted, damp hair.

"Sula will mend him up."

Dovie's tears flowed, glistening droplets mingling with crimson-tinged sweat. "It's not fair, Bert. He were only learnin' us to read."

"I know, Dovie."

"Master'll be mad. Monty's his best man."

It was a known fact that secret schools were operating in Savannah—whites teaching slaves; slaves teaching slaves—all illegal, all punishable by law.

John Paul Winston had taught Big Monty to cipher and read, as it was beneficial to his job, but it was illegal, too. Winston had no idea Monty was sharing his gift with his enslaved brethren at a secret school in his off hours. Now, Monty had been discovered and immediately punished.

The wagon rolled to a stop. "You get the master, Dovie. I'll go find Old Sula. She'll make a poultice."

Within minutes, John Paul Winston was at the shack, leaning over Monty as Sula applied a soothing poultice. Big Monty stared at the wall, his eyes glazed.

A scarlet flush crept up the master's neck as he surveyed the damage done to his slave's back. "How long have you been going to the secret school?"

"Some months, sir," Dovie answered, stroking Big Monty's cheek.

"Did you know it was forbidden?"

"Yes, sir."

"Why was Monty helping?"

"Everyone was wantin' to read. Books. The Bible, sir."

Sula straightened. "I'll change the poultice in a bit. Stops bleedin' and kills the pain."

Winston lightly touched Monty's shoulder.

"This won't go unnoticed, Monty. Unlawful or not."

A growl came from Monty's throat.

"I didn't hear, Monty. Say it again."

"You, too, sir."

Under Sula's care, Big Monty healed and resumed his chores with his former vigor. But the ridges on his back remained raised and angry, a legacy of his desire to pass on the blessing of reading.

Before long, Big Monty, Dovie, and Bert were gone during off hours again. Their absence was noticed by their owner, who correctly surmised they were attending the slave school, so great was their desire to read.

Winston became obsessed with a desire to find the school, but what did he propose to do if he did? Deny his chattel the same privilege he had already illegally granted to Monty? Bring his property safely home?

Finally, unable to resist the compulsion to look but one more time, Winston trailed Dovie and Bert into Savannah. After stabling the wagon, Bert and Dovie set out on foot. Winston followed at a distance, watching as they ducked into an alley and then through a doorway.

Winston followed and knocked. The door opened a mere sliver.

"May I help you?"

"May I come in?"

Big Monty appeared, pulled Winston in, and shut the door.

"Why are you here?"

"I came to see."

Ten pairs of eyes peered at Winston.

"You must leave, sir. You'll get us whipped."

"Please. Let me see the fruit of your labor." Winston hesitated. "Of my labor."

A Bible was produced. *"In the beginning was the Word—"* [1]

The door burst open. Two soldiers and a man in a black robe entered Everyone stared in frightened silence.

The black-frocked man addressed Winston. "Good sir, are you aware that this is an unlawful assembly, and furthermore, it's illegal to teach blacks to read."

"He's here for a recital, as it were," said Monty.

"Are you the teacher?"

"Yes, sir."

The soldiers seized Monty, dragging him into the alley.

"Unpleasant bit of business." The black-robed man pursed his lips in an expression of disgust. "I am sorry you were brought into this, sir. On your way, the rest of you."

"No! Stop," commanded Winston. "Let him go. I'll take it."

"Sir?"

"I said I'll take the whipping. Leave him be."

A chorus arose from the slaves, soldiers, and robed man, but Winston was adamant. He removed his overcoat and pulled his shirt from his trousers.

The tears rolled down Monty's cheek as Winston took each stripe.

. . . *and dwelt among us* . . . [2]

~·~

[1] John 1:1 (KJV)
[2] John 1:14b (KJV)

Remember, Read My Heart

LINDA WATSON OWEN

My Child, when sorrow covers you,
When every hope departs,
Though faith may seem to be afar,
Remember, read My Heart.

When you feel lost and all alone,
And suffer fear's dread darts,
Temptation will say I have gone,
But you can read My Heart.

For in your time of deepest need
You must this promise hold.
I love you more than words can say
More than can e'er be told.

I carry you within my breast.
Each hurt you bear, I feel.
And though all else may turn to dust,
My care for you is real.

So weather faithfully the storms
That tear and dash apart
Each remnant of your earthly life.
Remember, read My Heart.

Fret not to understand the why
Of losses you must bear.
For there will come a Time, you'll see,
When I make all things fair.

Now rest your head upon my arm,
And we will bear the pain.
Though dark the night and steep the way,
I with you will remain.

Don't trust the weakness of dim sight
For I the course will chart.
And when you fear you are alone,
Remember, read My Heart.

*"How priceless is your unfailing love!
Both high and low among men
find refuge in the shadow of your wings."*
Psalm 35:7

Book Worm

ELAINE TAYLOR

*F*EELING A LITTLE PECKISH, Book Worm perused his extensive library in search of something to nibble. It was a good thing his parents had been wise investors of their vast and impressive wealth. They had sacrificed and scrimped, dining on *Reader's Digest Condensed Books* and terrible novels. They wanted their only child to have the absolute best; hence his rather expensive tastes.

Book Worm had been known to devour entire series in one sitting, especially children's books. They were so sweet and delicious, with melt in your mouth yumminess, that he was constantly restocking his library with *The Little House on the Prairie* books, *The Chronicles of Narnia*, everything by Alcott, the *Oz* collection, and countless others.

I think it's too early for something sweet, he thought. *Perhaps something a little heartier.*

He was rather fond of *Treasure Island*, but it always left him with a terrible thirst due to its saltiness. His eyes skimmed over the many titles on the library shelves.

The Jungle Book.
The Swiss Family Robinson
Black Beauty
Rascal
At the Palace Gates
Follow My Leader
My Side of the Mountain
National Velvet
The Island of the Blue Dolphins . . .
Book Worm sighed. They were all wonderful.
Harry Potter
Artemis Fowl
Anne of Green Gables . . .

It was overwhelming trying to choose something.

Bronte

Austin

Dumas

Poe . . .

Not Dickens; his writing gave Book Worm heartburn . . . and definitely nothing by James Fenimore Cooper. They gave him gas.

Perhaps he should look in another bookcase, but which one? There were bookcases for travel, history, biographies, poetry, Shakespeare, mysteries, short stories, and countless others.

Then Book Worm spied the farthest case on the farthest wall—antiques. Now, the books on these particular shelves were not about antiques or collecting antiques. These books *were* antiques. His parents had scoured thrift stores and garage sales for tomes that were out of print or one-of-a-kind. These books were meant to be admired, not eaten.

(In case you didn't realize it, a book worm reads what he eats and eats what he reads.)

By now, Book Worm was downright hungry. He glanced upon a huge book marked as *The Holy Bible.*

How intriguing! he thought. *What does that mean? What is it about? How does it taste?* He hastily grabbed it off the shelf and tentatively crunched a corner. *Mmmmmm! Is that honey in the pages?*

He quickly gobbled up the whole thing, belched loudly, and slowly slid to the floor with a dreamy expression on his face. What a wondrous concoction of flavors and texture—lush sweetness and tart bitterness, tempered by a sprinkling of salt, as if from tears. Sure, the "begats" had been a little dry, but not overwhelmingly so. In fact, he had never eaten anything like it in his entire life.

Book Worm felt incredibly satisfied, yet at the same time, he was ravenous for more. He jumped up to search his library for another Bible, but another was not to be found.

Quickly, he ran to his favorite bookseller and bought every single Bible they had in stock:

Life Application

Amplified

The Message

Wuest Expanded Translation

New International Version

American Standard Version
Good News Translation
King James Version . . .
Book Worm bought them all.

Now every day, along with his ordinary fare, Book Worm munches a Bible or two and has become the healthiest, wealthiest, wisest book worm the village has ever seen. He happily tells others of this wonderful book and encourages them to taste it for themselves. With a gleam in his eye, he promises they will never feel hungry or thirsty again.

From Out of the Dark Sea

JOE HODSON

It was pitch dark on the beach. Fear nearly beat a hole in my chest and drowned out the roar of the waves punching the shore. Sand filled my shoes as we ran, making them like weights tied to my numb legs. The salt in the air tore at my lungs like a million microscopic lacerations. Any minute, the police could arrive.

"Hurry," Yingjie whispered.

Forty of us, dressed in dark clothes, were camouflaged by the blackness of the night. Each of us carried oversized pillowcases the women had made. Swiftly, silently we rushed to where the water meets the sand, our eyes scanning the open sea for the slightest flicker of a flashlight. There were forty of us in our church.

"Look!" said Tao, trying to hush his excitement. "A light! I see it!"

It looked like a dot; a twinkling star swimming in the black waters.

"Shh! Be quiet!" said Guang, our pastor. "Okay, everyone, get out into the water up to your waist. They should wash up very soon."

For three years, without ceasing, our church had prayed for this night. The water was cold but my body did not notice. As the water pulled at my ankles and legs, my heart shouted prayers of thanksgiving to God. A wave knocked me down. Salt water rushed up my nose and filled my mouth. Something unseen cut me, but I still held onto the pillowcase. I dragged myself back up and kept pushing toward the light shining from the distant rowboat. The Holy Spirit rose up inside of me, and I sang hymns and gave praise to our Lord Jesus Christ.

"I found one!" Bo's voice was a whisper over the noise of the lapping water.

Something bumped my waist. A small, rectangular object was bobbing on the water in front of me. My hands reached out, picked it up, and felt its edges inside the waterproof package.

It was a Bible.

More Bibles emerged from the dark. Hundreds of them. With a burst of joy I swam out to meet an island of fifty or more. My arms scooped the packages from the water and dropped them into the pillowcase. Salty tears and seawater blurred my vision as I hummed worship songs and praised Jesus for the glorious gift of His Word.

When there were no more Bibles to be found, we let the waves carry us back to land, where we threw the bags of Bibles onto the bed of a waiting, old, farm truck. We then watched as the truck pulled off, headlights unlit and a canvas tarpaulin hiding our "catch" from view. No police were in sight.

"Praise our Christian brothers and sisters overseas," I said to Bo. "Thank you, Lord. Praise your name! Now a thousand more of our brothers can read God's Word!"

Flooded with what felt like a million emotions, I hugged Bo as hard as I could. Our bodies were unequipped to contain the emotions that had taken hold of us, sending us to the ground. The moonlight revealed tears streaming down Bo's face. He looked heavenward, lifted his arms, and began to pray quietly, but powerfully, there on the sand. He prayed for our persecutors and for the government that imprisoned and executed us—the underground Christian church and Bible smugglers.

The Lord had shone His blessing on our faithful obedience.

In another hour the sun would rise and dissolve the night. It was time for each of us to leave for our homes, and anxiously await the next Bible drop-off.

Will You Walk Into My Parlor?

SALLY HANAN

SHE SITS IN THERE, in her white brick room beside the highway. The painted words on her outer wall call out to drivers like me:

Psychic Readings

The letters curl at the ends like beckoning fingers, luring me in to see my future spread out on her lacy table.

> *"Will you walk into my parlor?"*
> *said the Spider to the Fly,*
> *'Tis the prettiest little parlor*
> *that ever you did spy"*

One building down from her is the collision center. Their advertising is less enticing—a '70s Oldsmobile has been purposefully crashed into a fake wall, and there is no sign of it ever recovering. Does she realize the irony of her location?

> *"The way into my parlor*
> *is up a winding stair,*
> *And I have many curious things*
> *to show you when you are there."*

I drive by her shack of divinity twice a week on my way to church. I drive by tonight, and push my usual judgmental *pshaw* through my lips.

That's when I hear: *PRAY for her.*

> *"Oh no, no," said the Fly,*
> *"to ask me is in vain;*
> *For who goes up your winding stair*
> *can ne'er come down again."*

I push back on the steering wheel in surprise. *But God, wouldn't that . . . but don't I have to* LIKE *someone before I pray for them? And besides, what if I'm sucked in to her netherworld of evil?*

With a sideways glance (just in case she sees me looking), I check the outside of her devilish hut to see if I'm missing something.

My mind heads for the runway and begins to speed up.

> *"Oh no, no," said the little Fly,*
> *"for I've often heard it said*
> *They never, never wake again,*
> *who sleep upon your bed!"*

SCENARIO 1:

I sneak up on the place in the dark of night and walk around the psychic walls seven times. On the stroke of midnight I whip out my gold (well, gold-colored) ram's horn, blow for all I'm worth, and the walls fall down.

Voila!

She has no den of iniquity in which to serve.

The brain cells turn faster.

SCENARIO 2:

I curse the place.

It disappears in a horrible fire, and all of her fiendish instruments collect in the puddled ashes. (The lace tablecloth should catch the flames particularly nicely.)

Voila!

She has no occultist base from which to spread her poison.

Smoke is coming out of my ears.

> *"Oh no, no," said the little Fly,*
> *"kind sir, that cannot be,*
> *I've heard what's in your pantry,*
> *and I do not wish to see!"*

SCENARIO 3:

Yelling in tongues, I storm into the stronghold of Satan. I point my 600-page, gold-leafed Bible toward her bosom and yell, "Be gone, ye spirits of darkness."

Instantly she slumps to the floor, while the smell of sulphur creeps out of the room on all fours.

Voila!

She opens one eye and murmurs, "Wow, you are so awesome!"

We have gray matter take off.

> *"Sweet creature," said the Spider,*
> *"you're witty and you're wise;*
> *How handsome are your gauzy wings,*
> *how brilliant are your eyes!"*

SCENARIO 4:

I do what God has asked me to do and begin to pray for her.

⁓ꜱꜰꜱ⁓

I stop at the lights and check my teeth in the mirror.

I think I'll go with #3.

> *He dragged her up his winding stair,*
> *into his dismal den*
> *Within his little parlor—*
> *but she ne'er came out again!*

Pictures form. In my mind, I pull up beside her red Mazda that's parked by the front door. With cupped hand I lean my eyes into the car's back window to see a child's car seat belted in place. Fast food bags litter the floor.

I see myself entering to find a foyer of sorts—pink frills surround the solitary seat cushion, and a granddaughter's school drawing is pressed to the wall with a thumbtack.

A hand appears through the curtain of beads, followed by a large maternal body. "Hello, sweetie. You here to have your fortune read?" Her smile is one of heartache and struggle.

> *Unto an evil counselor*
> *close heart, and ear, and eye,*
> *And take a lesson from this tale*
> *of the Spider and the Fly.*

I stop the car and breathe. The pictures fade.
God, I'm so sorry.
And I begin to pray.

> *A word that's fitly spoken*
> *can cut through deepest bone,*
> *Lord take me from your quiver,*
> *and shoot this arrow home.*

~~~~~

The Spider and the Fly by Mary Howitt (1799-1888)
published 1829.

~~~~~

Editor's Note:
In *Will You Walk into My Parlor?* Sally's wonderful sense of humor combines
with her strong message to deliver the punch we have come to expect from
this talented writer. Although not quite lost in a good book, she definitely
communicated a very different type of "reading," which was the topic we gave
our writers for this section. As always, the creativity of these authors takes us in
many delightful directions, and this was one slight sidetrack I'm sure you will
have enjoyed. I know I did.

Turning the Tide

Karen Elengikal

*T*EARS GLISTENED IN THE flickering candlelight as they rolled down Daniel's cheeks before disappearing into the locks of his graying beard. It was always the same whenever he held the ancient parchments written by the patriarchs and the prophets. Trembling with deep emotion, he brought the aging document to his lips. With tenderness and awe he kissed the scroll; a kiss that poignantly demonstrated the passion of heart for his desolated homeland and for the purposes of Yahweh to be fulfilled. Unable to contain the secrets and longings of his heart, fervent prayer escaped his lips.

Tonight Daniel could sense the presence of the Lord. Angels assigned to open revelation waited, poised at his side. The room glowed in the illuminated blue light of the Shekinah presence of Israel's Holy One. A tryst with history was to be wrought. It was no ordinary night.

Slowly, reverently, Daniel unrolled the scroll of Jeremiah the prophet. Instantly, his mind revisited his dreadful passage from the Beloved Land, to here—heathen Babylon—his place of exile. Long years had since passed in captivity, but the memory of the burning ruins of Jerusalem had never faded.

Lost in thought, Daniel retraced his abduction from Jerusalem and the irreparable tearing of his heart at the knowledge that he would never see his homeland again.

Reliving the emotional upheaval, Daniel remembered the qualms he felt for the uncertain future he faced and his grief-laden prayers on that terrible journey. The prayers that birthed the resolve in his heart to serve the Lord despite the shame of exile . . .

The Palace Watchman's call announcing the second quarter of the night brought Daniel back to the present. Unseen, angels overshadowed Daniel, their hands on his, guiding him to the appointed passage of the prophet's words. Daniel began to read the Hebrew characters.

Barak was a good scribe, he mused. Despite the pressure of dangerous times, he faithfully transcribed Jeremiah's prophecies.

Drawing nearer and extending their swords toward the heavens, the angels spread their wings across Daniel as he read the Scriptures. There were to be no interruptions as this man, highly esteemed of the Lord, was appointed to gain understanding into future mysteries and the destiny of nations. As the night wore on, Daniel's lavishly appointed chamber continued to be visited by Heavenly Messengers, including the arrival of Gabriel.

Totally absorbed, Daniel soundlessly mouthed the inspired words, "This is what the LORD says: 'When seventy years are completed for Babylon, I will come to you and fulfill my gracious promise to bring you back to this place. For I know the plans I have for you,' declares the LORD, 'plans to prosper you and not to harm you, plans to give you hope and a future. Then you will call upon me and come and pray to me, and I will listen to you. You will seek me and find me when you seek me with all your heart. I will be found by you,' declares the LORD, 'and will bring you back from captivity. I will gather you from all the nations and places where I have banished you,' declares the LORD, 'and will bring you back to the place from which I carried you into exile.'" [1]

Revelation struck Daniel's heart as if a raging fire had ignited within his soul. "The seventy years has been completed," he whispered with rasped breath. "Israel must now return from captivity and be re-establish as a nation . . . the Messiah, the Anointed One, must be born in Israel . . ."

The scroll fell from Daniel's trembling hands and landed with a thud on the table. Seized with desperate urgency, he fell to his knees in agonized petition.

"O Lord, the great and awesome God, who keeps his covenant of love with all who love him and obey his commands . . ." [2]

Gabriel turned to another Messenger. "Go!" he commanded. "Tell Michael the news. Daniel has read the prophecy and revelation has been imparted. He has understood his path and has begun his intercession. The battle to turn the tide of Israel's history has begun!"

"O Lord, listen! O Lord, forgive! O Lord, hear and act! For your sake, O my God, do not delay, because your city and your people bear your Name . . ." [3]

~⸙~

Based on Daniel Chapter 9
[1] Jeremiah 29:10-14
[2] Daniel 9:4
[3] Daniel 9:19

Bookworms and Blueberries

ROBYN BURKE

"MOM, WHAT DOES 'I-DEE-LICK' MEAN?"
I looked up from my bread dough to meet the chocolate-brown eyes of my youngest daughter. Slightly confused by what could only be incorrect pronunciation, I requested she spell it.

"I-D-Y-L-L-I-C," she said.

"Oh, 'idyllic.' It means peaceful or calm, pleasant." I paused, thinking. "I spent an idyllic afternoon in the hammock."

Satisfied, Tessa returned to her book, and I to the pounding of dough.

Tessa was a reader. While her older brother and sister, Todd and Tara, were usually found outside chasing butterflies or playing catch, I could count on finding Tessa curled up in a chair—book in one hand, the other one twisting a lock of hair.

I certainly didn't mind; I was an avid reader myself. Todd and Tara were too, but they much preferred the outdoor activities of the farm and helping their dad. Save the book reading for evenings when daylight was gone, or when the weather was too unpleasant to play outside.

Ours was a good life, this one my husband and I had carved out on the old McGregor Farm. Country kids, both of us, we couldn't think of a better place to raise a family. We doled out chores along with discipline and manners. It was the way our parents raised us and their parents had raised them.

Out of the corner of my eye, I watched my eight-year-old's mouth work its way around another unfamiliar word. My heart surged with pride for the independent streak that would not allow her to ask for help until she had exhausted her own efforts.

Sure enough, I saw her face alight with comprehension before she sank back into her little world.

I moved the bread dough to the warming oven and wiped my hands. "Tess, tear yourself away from your book a minute and come take a walk with me."

She groaned but obeyed.

While I was glad she loved to read, I worried that my little bookworm wasn't getting enough physical activity. As we made our way down the worn path to the garden, I looked closely at her. In the sunlight, I noticed dark circles under her eyes and wondered how long she'd stayed awake the night before, reading under the covers. I circled my arm around her shoulders and drew her close. Instantly she stood straighter.

As usual, it had been a busy, productive summer, and perhaps I had been too busy to really pay attention to my quiet, compliant child. With a rowdy thirteen-year-old son and a precocious eleven-year-old daughter clamoring for my time, Tessa was the easy one.

Maybe too easy, and too often overlooked.

I resolved to spend some extra time with Tessa before school resumed next month.

We reached the blueberries and knelt together as I handed Tessa one of the buckets that rested against the fencepost. For some time we picked berries in companionable silence, enjoying the plinking of plump ripe fruit as it landed in the pails. Sunlight danced across the burnished red of the blueberry bush. The cooing of a dove lulled us.

"Mom?" Tessa's voice broke the stillness. "Is this an i-dyl-lic moment?"

Sitting back on my heels, I studied her small face for a moment, brushing back a strand of hair so I could better see her eyes.

A memory floated to the surface like a picture from a storybook. I was a child, picking vegetables from the garden with my mother. It was a memory awash in sunshine—fragrant and rich.

Tessa grinned, and a wave of love rushed over me—a love so fierce, so pure. I wished I could freeze-frame this moment.

"Idyllic? Yes, Tessa, I believe it is."

Outside the Dome

T.F. CHEZUM

"GOOD EVENING, CAMPERS. IT'S a balmy 43.2 degrees Celsius, and methane levels are stable. Make sure you're sealed up and your breathers are clear or you'll be goin' home in the back of the cruiser."

Rory squatted near the excavation. "So, what do we got?"

"The probe's just starting to transmit." Chrissie adjusted the instrument panel, her voice muted through the speaker in her environmental suit.

Candi moved near the work area.

"We're at 54.29 meters and descending." Chrissie toggled a switch on the top of the unit. "And we've landed at 58.37."

Candi clapped her hands.

"First dig, kid?" Rory put his hand on her back.

She nodded.

"Don't get your hopes up," he said. "Never find any ancient hieroglyphics to interpret down in these holes."

"Numbers coming in." Chrissie typed commands on her console. "Temperature 16.7. Atmosphere, methane . . ." She gazed at her monitor, disbelief flashing in her eyes. "Wait, I—"

"Just give me the readings, Chrissie," Rory huffed. "And where's the video?"

"Methane, hydrogen, sulfur hydride all trace amounts, but this doesn't make sense. Nitrogen 76 percent, oxygen 22. I'll recalibrate."

"Don't bother." Rory knocked on the face shield of his helmet. "As long as we have our air supply it don't really matter what's down there."

Chrissie typed a series of codes.

"It's definitely a large cavern. Let's see . . ."

She smacked the side of the unit with her glove-covered palm. "And we have video."

The monitor flickered and static-filled images flashed across the screen. The three watched with great intent as rock formations and other vague shapes passed.

"It's all rubble." Rory stood up. "Let's pack it up and call it a day."

"Wait!" Candi pointed to the screen. "Did you see that? Chrissie, pan left."

The technician manipulated the joystick.

"*There!* You see it?" Candi's excitement could not be contained. "It's a structure."

Rory glanced at the picture. "It's just a cave wall."

"No, it's not," she protested. "It has some kind of symbols on it. We have to go down and check."

"Oh, come on," he grumbled. "Let's just complete the reports and head home."

"It is protocol, boss," Chrissie chimed in. "We go in whenever there's any doubt."

"What doubt?" he hissed.

"How 'bout the atmosphere readings?"

⁓≈≋✦≋≈⁓

The shuttle rumbled to a stop near the probe. The three workers stepped into the dark, dusty environment. Rory turned on his helmet light and surveyed the area. "Watch the manifolds, they get a little hot."

"I'm getting the same readings." Chrissie tapped the portable sensors. "This air's breathable."

"You keep that helmet on," Rory barked. "C'mon, let's get this wrapped up."

"There it is!" Candi ran across the cavern. Rory and Chrissie gave chase.

"I knew it." Candi gestured. "Look."

The pursuers skidded to a stop, their mouths agape.

"Look at the beautiful sculpting—the real wood. I've only seen pictures." Candi bounded up to the small building. "This shows there could've been life outside the domes." She stepped inside.

"It don't show nothin', kid." Rory waved his arms in disgust. "It's just an old dome that was destroyed in the cataclysm."

"Then how do you explain the air?" Chrissie inquired.

"Don't have to. No one's gonna know." He leaned against the probe. "Anomalies don't get reported."

"This is more than just . . ." Chrissie's eyes grew with disbelief. "You alter the reports?" She stepped away. "You don't want people to know what's out here."

"We're livin' in a dome that barely supports us as it is." He paced the silt-covered ground. "We should be lookin' for ways to improve our lives now, but all we're doin' is chasin' the past."

"Haven't you ever wondered where we came from?" Chrissie pleaded. "Dreamed that maybe we could find life outside the domes?"

"There's nothin' we need in these dead caves," Rory snarled.

"They'll find out, eventually," she whispered.

"You can't prove anything." He grabbed her shoulder.

"I have proof." Candi walked from the structure, a book held in her trembling hands.

"What's this?" He grabbed it from her and flipped through the pages. "It's all gibberish."

He dropped it.

Candi bent and picked up the book. "It's the ancient language." Confidence was building in her voice.

Chrissie gazed at the tiny symbols. "It hasn't been used since—"

"And who's gonna translate it?" Rory blurted, a smirk on his face.

"I can read it." Candi opened to the first page.

"In the beginning, God . . ."

PART FOUR

Crafted with Love

Shavings

MID STUTSMAN

*A*GOLDEN GLOW FRAMED THE cedar doorposts of a Mediterranean-style mansion, where a lone figure stood in the entryway, casting a shadow across the marble tiles of the floor. When he entered, the light followed, permeating the room with soft rays.

The interior of the home exuded the warmth of his handiwork. He ran his hand over each piece of furniture, crafted to perfection from exotic rosewood and mahogany, and accented with gold leaf filigree. Botanical prints, done in low relief, framed the arches of the interior doorways. Pale watercolors were brushed over the surface of the designs to make them stand out even more. Terrazzo floors swirled with the hues of a misty sunrise and gleamed in the light of his presence as he walked through the rooms. Scenes from special moments had been faithfully etched into each tile—a unique reminder of a life graced with love.

Time was not an issue; no expense was spared. There was an elegant simplicity to everything he made, from the recessed bookshelves in the library, to the desk for drawing and writing. Carved wood trim outlined the windows. Exposed timbers highlighted the vaulted ceilings. Every inch of the mansion bore his imprint of excellence.

He looked around, pleased with his progress. There was only one more project he needed to finish for the garden courtyard.

The fragrances of frankincense, myrrh, and spices blended with the air rising from the aromatic shavings on the floor. Like a cloud of incense, it mingled with the carpenter's sweat and blood, reminding him of another day, another piece of wood.

He willed the image away and continued to work, his skilled hands moving deftly over the teak boards on his bench. He shaped them to exact measurements, breathing life into every stroke. Each curl of wood falling to the floor took with it a whispered prayer, and a promise that no one would ever have to go through what he had experienced so very long ago.

He picked up a small box, took out his carving tools, and inscribed a name at the top of the finished arch. When he was done gilding the letters, he hand-rubbed the structure to a soft patina, and set it against the wall.

He gathered his tools, cleaned his workspace. The shavings went into the deep pockets of his apron.

Outside, the courtyard reflected the elegant theme of the mansion. A teak table and benches graced the terracotta patio. Large stone jars, planted with trees and ornamental grasses, stood in groupings of three around the edge. Beyond them could be heard the lighthearted melody of water splashing into a hidden pool. Fragrant flowers and herbs lined the curved walkway leading to an unfinished entrance, where espaliered fruit trees edged the low garden wall on either side of the opening.

The carpenter positioned the arch in the empty space, sliding the posts into the bases he had prepared earlier. He patted the sides of the structure and scattered the shavings on the ground beneath. Taking a few steps back, he checked to see if the arch was straight.

"Perfect," he whispered.

He unrolled the blueprints of my life and looked at the mansion one more time. "It won't be long . . ."

～✻～

"In My Father's house are many mansions:
If if were not so, I would have told you.
I go to prepare a place for you."
John 14:2 (KJV)

Cajun Peace in de Valley

MARILEE WILLIAMS ALVEY

ROUBLE STARTED WID TWO churches in Lafayette, Louisiana. De guilty know der shame.

Every year de Methodists would have a Craft Fair. Dey was methodical, dem Methodists, and none more than Etienne Boudreax, who was in charge of de fair dat fateful year. Etienne was de kind who could put hammers, plows, and all sorts on her wall and make it look like barn chic. Tried dat myself once. Folks came in and aksd, "Whazzat washboard doin' on yer wall?"

Etienne had chosen "Peace in de Valley" as her theme. Things was crankin' up right fine. Church ladies planned to sell mudbugs served on newspapers, but dey was puttin' on airs and callin' dem 'crayfish' like dem Nawthern parishes. Dey figured dis could save on buyin' paper plates. Course folks was welcome to make wit' de Tabasco, as well.

Crafts came flyin'. Tall stuffed rabbits that hid de vacuum cleaner so's you could keep it out and people'd never see it. Tissue box covers shaped like little houses. De whole nine yards. Folks was pretty hepped up about it and ready to stand in line.

Der was a fly in de ointment: Cleoma Tibaudau. She'd decided to hold de Baptist Church Raffle on de same weekend. Bein' only a block away from de Methodist Church, dis wouldn't float. She put up a ad in de paper. Turns out "Puttin' on de Glitz" would have men in tuxes parkin' cars. 'Round dese parts, if'n you can get a man to put on a tux, folks will come and see it, I guarantee.

Not only dat, but Cleoma done advertised that der would be dose little horse dovrays: crackers wid spray cheese on 'em, spam kaybobs, and such. I ain't lyin'. She even advertised a sit you down dinner. To hear 'em tell 'bout it over at de Methodist Church, you'da thot she'd installed a drive-through tarot card window in her home.

"Peace in de Valley" my foot! It was now "War in de Trenches."

Next ting you knowd, Etienne hired a String Or-chestra. Sorta. Closest ting we got in Lafayette is a Blue Grass jug band.

She found some fella who had a cotton candy machine and got him goin'. Den she found someone who could bend balloons into stupid stuff, and someone who could juggle heavy wood pins.

Cleoma got wind of dat and de fur did fly. She didn't like dat, no. She bought a bunch o' sheets and got out her BeDazzler™ and bedazzled jewels all around dem sheets, den pulled 'em back 'til de church entry look like some kinda hoochy-koochy palace. She glued glitter over everythin'. Nobody could sit but der backside was shinin' like a big ol' billboard. The Baptists was truly standin' up for Jesus dat week.

Etienne wasn't just standin' still. No. Eleven at night she was sneakin' down de street, placin' plastic footprints from de Baptist Church to de Methodist Church. After dat, she was tired but it had made her de confidence dat she was ready.

Back at da bayou, Cleoma had got a old Mr. Microphone and some big speakers, mounted dem on a truck , and as soon as day broke, commenced to "take de show on de road." Two good ol' Baptist boys was shoutin' out. De way dey was braggin' 'bout der event, you'd a thot salvation was through works.

Cleoma began liftin' up dem footprints, one by one. She made mad. She had a group o' good Baptists followin' right behind, lookin' every bit like mad ol' Philistines.

"Y'all cease and desist, in de name o' Jesus!" she proclaim. You'd a thot she was doin' an exorcism.

De blue grass band done froze.

De fella throwin' pins got off-stride.

Dem pins knocked over de vat o' mudbugs, splat.

De fella foldin' up balloons, he done slipped on dat mudbug water and went kaboom.

De guy makin' da cotton candy, he make like a statue wid his mouth hangin' open and forgot to catch up de cotton candy.

Fibers was floatin'. Kids started throwin' mudbugs. Sister, Revelations done come to life.

Cleoma came at Etienne, gave her a pair o' eyes, den slipped on de mudbugs. Etienne, de good Christian, tried to catch her. Dey ended up in a pile, laughin' and laughin'. Folks jest joined in, slippin' and slidin'. Looked like one of dem mosh pits.

All went home dat night sayin' might as well quit. "Peace in de Valley" done beat 'em all.

Crafts 4 Kids

KENN ALLAN

Time to spend but none to waste,
Paints and dyes (all water based),
Whitish globs of tasty paste—
These are things you'll need . . .

Scissors honed with rounded tips,
Crayons, chalk, and paper clips,
Kisses, hugs, and bandage strips
When hearts and elbows bleed.

Buttons, thread, and candy bars,
Sable brushes, jelly jars,
Rhinestones shaped like golden stars,
Can decorate the years . . .

Or perhaps, as some prefer,
Wheels that spin and gears that whir,
Pots of mud with sticks to stir
Will serve as souvenirs.

Birthday candles (slightly charred),
Glitter from a Christmas card,
Patience purchased by the yard
For awkward questions braved . . .

Macaroni (not with cheese),
Blossoms gathered from the trees,
Lofty giggles on the breeze
Are treasures to be saved.

If working with divine designs,
Take care to stay within the lines,
And make sure righteousness defines
The items you've compiled . . .

And when your skills are wearing thin,
A spray of love will seal them in—
Well, are you ready to begin?
Let's build a happy child!

A Good Work

ANN GROVER

THOMAS COLLYER HAD A lot on his mind. There was Sunday's sermon to ponder. A baptism one week hence, a wedding in three days, and the midsummer's fair in a fortnight. Most importantly, however, his beloved wife was laboring with their first child in the nearby vicarage.

"She's coming along, Vicar." Mrs. Blackburn had brought him a pot of tea and a plate of buttered scones earlier. "When it's time, I'll fetch you."

Thomas ran anxious fingers through his hair until it stood straight up, and he nibbled at the scones, crumbs littering his vest. He tried to concentrate, but his thoughts were like feathers in the wind. Maybe a turn about the churchyard would relieve his mind.

The air was damp, mist wending through the headstones, dew lying heavy on the grass between the rows. *A dreary day to be born*, he thought. He glanced toward the vicarage, but it was silent and taciturn. He pulled his watch from his pocket; the hands hadn't moved since the last time he'd looked.

Thomas strolled around the back of the church, observing that weeds had overgrown some of the older graves, mossy scabs capping the stones. A work bee was in order.

"Vicar, it's best you come." Mrs. Blackburn's voice broke through Thomas's reverie, and he looked up expectantly. The housekeeper was already plodding through the sodden grass, and Thomas followed the stooped shoulders.

The vicarage was hushed. Thomas felt a prickle of fear as he ascended the stairs, knowing, yet afraid to know for certain.

"You have a daughter, Vicar. Alyce is dying. I'm very sorry."

Thomas did not hear. He was intent on the waxen face framed by damp curls. He tenderly touched Alyce's cheek. Her eyes fluttered open and soundless words came from her bloodless lips. Thomas bent closer.

"Care for her. Love you."

Thomas laid his head against her chilled hand. "Help us to trust Thy loved ones to Thy care . . ." He felt her life ebb away. *Help me.*

Gentle mewling came from the cradle by the bed. Thomas lifted his head. *Help me, God.*

~ ⚜ ~

The day of the funeral was sunny.

"I am the Resurrection and the Life . . . Hear our prayer."

"And let our cry come unto Thee."

On cue, tiny Elizabeth whimpered in Mrs. Blackburn's arms. Thomas sprinkled soil onto the coffin, as did the parishioners as their grieving vicar dismissed them. Several ladies tried to engage Thomas in conversations about wet nurses and mother care. Thomas walked on, deaf.

While Elizabeth slept, Thomas went through the layette, each item lovingly sewn, knitted, or crocheted by Alyce over the last few months. He examined each bootie, nightgown, and jacket, trying to understand the ties and buttons.

Later, while going through Alyce's work basket, Thomas found her final project. It was an embroidered infant's bonnet, tiny sprays of flowers on cotton, the embroidery incomplete, the brim and ties not yet attached. He would give it to Mrs. Blackburn for completion.

Yet . . .

Thomas held the bonnet to his cheek, trying to glean the lingering touch of his Alyce's fingers. He thought about the small life sleeping in the cradle, blissfully unaware.

Help me.

Clumsily, Thomas threaded the needle and knotted the thread. He pulled it through the cotton. Down again. One stitch. Up. Down again. Two stitches. A tear streaked down Thomas's face and soaked into the pristine fabric. He didn't know what to do. He searched through the basket for a guide. Nothing.

He continued the stitch he'd started. It was ungainly, not as graceful as Alyce's stitches. He changed colors and tried another stitch. It didn't work, not on the first attempt, not on the tenth, not after he marred the cloth with his blood.

After several more tries, he managed a lopsided imitation of Alyce's stitch, and he tried for another, faring better, although he snarled the thread twice. He determinedly made another.

Some of the stitches were beyond him, little buds of twisted thread. They'd have to wait until he had help.

~ ⚜ ~

Although she readily gave him guidance, it was a mystery to Mrs. Blackburn why the vicar finished the bonnet. It was greyed when it was completed several weeks later, and the bloodstain never entirely washed out.

To Thomas it was simple. Alyce had begun a work, and he'd finished it. Just as they'd begun a good work together in Elizabeth, and he'd complete it, too.

Help me, God.

Boys Don't Do Sewing

GREGORY KANE

~⚜~

THE DOOR SLAMMED AND heavy, thumping footsteps crossed the room. Winnie didn't need to look up to know the source of the disturbance. She continued with her needlepoint and waited for the explosion.

"Nan, I'm bored. There's nothing to do here."

"I know, dear. It's very sad."

"I'm serious, Nan," shouted Peter, her ten-year-old grandson. "There's nothing to do in this stupid house. You haven't even got cable. I told Dad he should have let me bring my PlayStation!"

Winnie smiled to herself but she still didn't look up. Her tapestry was coming along well and she hoped to finish it before the end of the week. Peter was only visiting for four days, but he seemed to have the attention span of a horsefly doped to the eyeballs with food additives and colorants. His grandfather had already abdicated all responsibility and had taken himself off fishing. Winnie had hoped Peter might like to go along, but the boy's only response had been "Borrrriinnng!"

"You could always come and help me with my needlepoint." Winnie didn't really have any expectation that Peter would agree, so she wasn't surprised by his immediate reaction.

"Nan, that is *plain* stupid!"

This was said in such a whiney voice that the old woman glanced up from her craft project.

Her grandson was standing with his legs askew, hands on hips, mouth open, tonsils quivering, and such a look on his face that you could imagine he had just been offered curried caterpillars in mayonnaise for breakfast.

"What's the problem, Peter dear?" she asked all innocence.

"Needlecraft is for girls," he insisted, coating each word with as much disgust and incredulity as he could muster.

"Oh, I didn't know that. I didn't realize that God was a girl."

"What do you mean?"

"Haven't you heard, dear? The Bible is full of sewing, knitting, woodcraft, all that sort of thing."

Peter stared suspiciously at his grandmother. Then he walked over to an empty chair and sat down. "Go on," he said. "This is a joke, isn't it? No, let me guess, David didn't kill Goliath with a sling, he used a crochet hook."

Winnie set down her needlepoint and grinned at the young man opposite her. Peter's father, her son, was a church minister, and she knew that Peter liked showing off his Bible knowledge. "Well now, where shall I begin?" she mused. "I suppose that Bezalel would be a good place to start."

"Where?" asked Peter.

"Not where, but who. Bezalel appears in the book of Exodus when he helped Moses make the Tabernacle."

"That was the holy tent, wasn't it, Nan?" chipped in Peter, keen to prove that he really did know his Bible.

"That's right. The Holy Spirit gave him special abilities so he could work with wood, metal, and precious stones."

"But that's hardly needlepoint."

"True enough," Winnie agreed. "But his assistant, Oholiab, had skill in embroidery and weaving. And they were both men."

Peter thought about this for a moment. Then he launched his counter-attack. "Yes, Nan, but that doesn't mean God does girly stuff like tapestry."

Winnie lifted up one hand and began to count on her fingers. "The Psalmist says that God 'knit me together in my mother's womb' so He must knit. Isaiah says of Him, 'I have engraved you on the palms of my hands,' so God must do engraving. Isaiah also says, 'We are the clay, you are the potter,' so clearly God is into pottery."

Peter pulled a face. "Yeah, sure. And I suppose you'll say that God sews because the farmer went out to sow his seed?"

"I would, dear, but your Bible knowledge is obviously better than your spelling. But the Bible does say in Ecclesiastes that there is 'a time to rend, and a time to sew.'"

Peter looked at his grandmother with wary respect. "You sure do know your Bible. I suppose that's why Dad's so good."

"Practice, my boy, practice. Now what about helping me with my needlepoint?"

"No way, Nan," he replied. "I'm off to find a tree to climb."

Peter was halfway toward the door when he stopped and turned. "I don't suppose there's anything in the Bible about God playing computer games?"

Winnie thrust her chest forward, put her hands on her hips, and exclaimed in her best whiney voice, "Peter, that is *plain* stupid!"

Wonderfully Made

HELEN PAYNTER

*I*N APRIL, I HID hope in my bosom . . .
I worked open the bottom drawer of my oak dresser and pulled back the layers of tissue paper within. There lay waiting a bolt of white linen.

I lifted its solemn weight in my arms, and unfolded it reverently. Its crisp smell lingered like a blessing. The billowing whiteness, as I shook out the folds, diffused the sunlight into a soft pearlescent glow.

I heated the flat iron in the fire and pressed the damped fabric, its soft hiss accompanying my silent dreams.

I marked it with minute dabs of tailor's chalk and pressed willing scissors to their task.

In May, I felt a stirring within . . .
I creased the fabric into parallel folds, the slub softly abrading my fingers. With my finest needle I made tracks of invisible stitches to secure the folds. In patient silence, my hopes grew with my work.

In June, expectation began to blossom . . .
I selected palest cream thread and embroidered over the smocking. Loops and whorls; flowers and zigzags. The rise and fall of my needle matched my quiet breathing. I knew that both within and without something wonderful was being crafted.

In July, my ambition broadened . . .
With panels and darts I completed the bodice. The flat, formless pieces rose and took shape. I set in the sleeves with tiny stitches. The skirt fell in soft folds from the waistband. I backstitched and hemmed, neat lines of herring-bone covering the raw edges.

In August, I completed my masterpiece . . .

I embellished the hem and cuffs with subtle lace fashioned with the slenderest of threads. I took white silk buttons and ranked them in gentle salute down the center seam. I threaded the neckline with satin ribbons.

In September it was time to rest . . .

I pressed the dress with exquisite care, each pleat crisp, each crease smooth. Then I hung the dress beside the crib.

In silence, we waited.

In October, I held my first-born in my arms and kissed his butter-soft forehead. I held him to my breast and traced his tiny nails with my fingertips. His eyelashes were long—so long.

With feathering fingers I dressed him in his Christening dress and fastened the silk buttons behind him. I smoothed the folds over his tiny form and tied the ribbons in painstaking bows.

Then, baptizing him in my tears, I laid him tenderly in the cold earth.

～⚜～

Author's Note:

In 2013, infant mortality in much of the developed world was approximately 4.5 per 1,000 live births. In parts of Africa, the figure is twenty-five times as high.

Taught by a Nosegay

PATTY WYSONG

Let all bitterness, and wrath, and anger, and clamour,
and evil speaking, be put away from you, with all malice
Ephesians 4:31 (KJV)

FOR TEN YEARS I'VE been the chief craft-lady at my church, and I've made the centerpieces and favors for every Ladies' Spring Banquet, but not this year. Oh no, they went and asked some new lady to do them.

Secretly, I was hoping the banquet would come close to a flop so they'd see how much they need me, but no such luck. Inside the fellowship hall, all was calm and peaceful. Most of the seats were taken, too.

"Yoo-hoo! Vickie, you can sit with us."

I stifled a groan and painted on what I hoped was a pleasant smile. "Mrs. Milligan, how nice to see you tonight."

Mrs. Milligan was truly a dear soul, but she loved to talk. As I thought about it, though, I realized that was just what I needed—a chatty table where I could sit and stew.

"Aren't the centerpieces lovely? I was so disappointed when I heard they'd asked that new lady, Paula What's-her-name, to do them this year. They say she's had a hard time settling in, but that she's doing much better now. But you've always done such beautiful arrangements, dear, and it's become a highlight of the banquet for me. I still have my favors from past years that you made."

Mrs. Milligan may have liked to talk, but she did make me feel better.

"Will you look at these favors, Vickie, dear. What do you make of them?"

They were darling—silk nosegays tied with a bow so you could put them in a vase at home, but there was something glaringly wrong with them. Right in the middle was the ugliest little flower. I was astounded.

Was Paula out of her mind? Did she think that flower was pretty? How could she think to camouflage that with even a hundred other pretty ones?

Mrs. Milligan was interrupted by our pastor's wife, who was opening the banquet. "Good evening, ladies. Isn't it wonderful to be here tonight? Now, I don't want to keep dinner waiting, but I heard the buzz and thought I'd take care of one little thing before we go any further, since I'm sure you'll enjoy the dinner more once it's taken care of." She held up a larger version of the favors and pointed to a similarly ugly flower tucked in with all the pretty ones. "This is what's had y'all buzzing since you came in, isn't it?"

There was a loud murmuring of ladies agreeing.

"Well, do you know what this is?"

I could hear every lady silently screaming, "Yeah! It's an ugly flower!" But no one said a word since Paula What's-her-name was in the room, too.

"This is an ugly flower."

The ladies let go of the breaths they'd been holding.

"Well, it is, isn't it?"

This time there was no holding back. "Yes!"

"Can all these other pretty flowers hide this one? No, they can't. When I look at this nosegay, all I can see is this one ugly flower, and I know that's all y'all see, too."

The ladies were all laughing and agreeing with her.

"We're all like this nosegay, did you know that?"

The room quieted down.

"We can have all the pretty flowers in our lives, but if there's bitterness, or wrath, or anger, or clamor, or slander, or any malice in our life, it can never be camouflaged, no matter how many pretty flowers we use. If we don't get rid of the uglies, that will be all anyone ever sees—the ugliness.

"So, y'all do everyone a favor now. Get ahold of that ugly flower in your nosegay and pluck it out. Just ease it right out and toss it away." She pulled the ugly flower out of the large nosegay and tossed it over her shoulder.

Throughout the room, ladies pulled out their ugly flowers and laughingly tossed them over their shoulders, too.

"There! That's so much better. A life without bitterness, or slander, or whatever, is a beautiful life. Now, let's pray and ask God to do the same in our hearts and to bless this dinner."

Oh, Father, I silently prayed, *forgive me for becoming bitter and angry over not making the centerpieces and favors. Please remove that bitterness and anger, and make me beautiful.*

Intertwined

JOANNE MALLEY

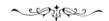

One day beyond the pearly gates
The Lord our God rejoiced,
Another child would walk the earth
And this is what He voiced . . .

"My hands, like tools, will mold your form
With threads of Heaven's fleece,
Each stitch I make, each part I craft
Reveals a masterpiece.

"Until you're born no one can see
The parts that I've combined,
And you will bear all that you need—
Three pieces intertwined.

"The first, your heart, will beat with love
One's given every man,
Though how you choose to nurture it
Remains in your own hands.

"The next, your mind, will hold the thoughts
Of what is right and true,
But if you disregard each one
My eyes will cry for you.

"The third, your soul, is empty 'til
You recognize I'm there,
It's then your being comes to life
And heaven sings this prayer . . .

'It's with great pride we do proclaim
Your fabric is elite,
Exalted is our Lord and God
For He's made you complete.

'Who you'll become was meant to be
No other's quite the same,
He took the time to craft just one
And now you'll bear His name.

'He placed you in your mother's womb
And as you grew, He beamed,
Your every part turned out just right—
Exactly how He dreamed.'"

And then the angels bowed to God
They praised His work that day,
He sat upon His splendid throne
And had these words to say . . .

"With hands, like tools, I molded you
Of heart and soul and mind,
Creator and His masterpiece—
Forever intertwined."

~⟐~

For you created my inmost being;
you knit me together in my mother's womb.
Psalm 139:13

Loving Ugly

LINDA GERMAIN

"So, WHAT'S THE EMERGENCY, sis?" Daisy's face showed concern as she walked through my door.

"Oh, Daisy," I whined. "Karl's mother is coming to visit, and since we moved I can't find the box."

"What box, Tulie?" All of us girls were named after flowers, but I was adamant about not being called Tulip.

"You know, the box where I hide all those tacky, crafty things my well-meaning mother-in-law sends. I usually wait until she is coming for a visit before I set them out. As soon as she leaves, they go back into storage."

Karl had let me know, in no uncertain terms, that he was staying out of it, but my precious older sister was willing to help.

"Let's hop to it," Daisy commanded, as she pulled on my arm. "We'll start at the top and work our way down."

"Thanks. What would I do without you?"

She didn't answer. I guess she had heard that line too many times before.

Together we climbed the steep stairs to the roomy attic. Sunshine poured through several of the tall windows.

"Okay, here's the plan." Daisy always said that first. She just loved to organize. "Which boxes are you sure are not the ones with the craft goodies?" She was already making sense with her calm demeanor and deductive reasoning.

Box by box, we searched for the one that would yield its tea cozies, dishwashing liquid bottle dresses, little house-shaped covers designed for every appliance imaginable, and painted wood signs with messages like "Welcome" and "Kiss the Cook."

A few hours later, with no success, we escaped to the kitchen for iced tea. I could see by the way she chewed her bottom lip that Daisy was beginning to work on Plan B.

"What . . ." she postulated with slow deliberation, "is the one thing she'd be most hurt not to see?"

That was a no-brainer. It had to be the lampshade she fashioned out of an old silk parachute. She stenciled all the different flowers representing my sisters and me. There were roses, lilacs, daisies, violets and tulips. Green was feathered around the bottom to look like grass, and on the top part, an extreme sky blue.

Daisy tried to suppress a giggle. "Do you have a picture of that one-of-a-kind decorator accessory?"

"Yes," I retorted to my smart-aleck sister, "I just happen to have that very thing." I stomped off to the den with what I hoped was a show of disgust at her complete enjoyment of my predicament.

When I returned with the evidence, she seemed to be dumbstruck. "Wow," she eventually managed. "It really is amazingly awful isn't it?"

"I told you, smarty-pants." I really needed to work on my attitude, but right now wasn't the time.

My sensible sibling changed back to detective mode. "How do you know this monstrosity means so much to her?"

"Well, for one thing, every time she comes for a visit, the first thing she says is, 'Oh my. I see you still have the lampshade . . . and in such a prominent spot, too.' Then she'll make reference to how well it has held up over the years."

"I would assume it stayed so nice because you whisked it away the second she left . . . right?"

I made a face, but I had to admit Daisy had a brilliant plan. She said she had some material and an old lampshade that could pass.

"We'll enlarge the picture and try to copy it exactly. She'll never notice the difference."

We stayed up all night re-creating until we were too dopey to see straight. By the time Karl pulled into the driveway with the woman whose feelings I was trying so hard to spare, the lamp was in full regalia and standing splendidly on the hall table. The look on her face spoke volumes. Her eyes were as big as crocheted waffle-iron covers.

"Oh, my dear Tulie. Have you still got that perfectly ghastly shade? I thought it would have died a natural death years ago. You must *really* love it."

I ran for my private prayer closet before I embarrassed us both. After I calmed down, revelation surprised me. No, I did not really love it, but I did *really love her.*

That was the best visit I can remember with the grandmother of my children. When we said goodbye, she whispered knowingly, "Please dump the silly thing."

Ah . . . free at last.

A Beautiful Design

Helen Curtis

I WONDER, HAVE YOU EVER stopped to look at a stained-glass window? I mean, really considered its beauty, the skill of the artist, the hours of planning and labor required to create it?

Each window is unique.

It begins as a vision that grows and forms in the mind of the artist, developing as he puts the design down on paper.

When he is satisfied that the design is very good, he turns each individual section into a stencil. Each section of glass is handmade by the artist; every hue is perfectly blended into the glass as it is melted, molded and cooled.

Following his original design, he hand-cuts the panes to the exact specifications. He carefully welds the lead joints together, and finally, he applies a cement-like substance to ensure every piece stays in place.

Once finished, the artist carefully places the work of art up against the very brightest of light sources, then stands back to survey his handiwork. Smiling with deep satisfaction, he declares it to be very, very good.

It is then tenderly packed and transported to its intended destination. There, secured in place, the light shines through and the picture is brought to life. Those who gaze upon it revel in its beauty and marvel at the artist's skill.

The Bible tells us that our lives have been planned in much the same way. We each began as a vision in God's omnipotent mind. We are not accidents of some cosmic explosion; God thought of every single one of us individually, personally—and He has a plan and a purpose for our existence.

Yes, the omnipotent creator of all of heaven and earth designed your blueprints, and mine. Using the DNA our lineage provided for us, He built unique masterpieces: you . . . you . . . and yes, you.

Let's once again consider the stained-glass window and its details. Some of the panes are beautifully colored—azure blues, magenta pinks, and sunny yellows. But I wonder, would these be as bright if they weren't set against the crimson reds, the midnight blues, the ink-stain blacks?

Our lives are not free from dark hues. Troubles come to us all—pain and suffering, loss of loved ones, unemployment, illness. Any number of things can cause us to question God's plan and design for our lives. "Surely, this can't be of God?" we cry. "This can't be part of His perfect design . . . can it?"

In all honesty, I'm not sure how to answer that, but what I can offer is reassurance that no matter what the circumstance, God our creator knows all about it, and we are in His thoughts constantly.

He sees our pain, He sees our tears, and He wants to be there for us, as our comfort.

> *You have searched me, Lord, and you know me.*
> *You know when I sit and when I rise;*
> *you perceive my thoughts from afar.*
> *You discern my going out and my lying down;*
> *you are familiar with all my ways.*
> Psalm 139:1-3

Just as the beauty of the stained-glass window is revealed by the light shining through, so it is with our lives as we allow the light of God's presence to shine through us. As we trust in Him in the midst of trials, people will gaze upon our inner beauty and ask where our strength comes from.

As we share of the faith we have in our loving, caring God—the Creator God who thinks of us more deeply than any other being—they will consider the skill of the Master's hand. This might not be the moment they come to faith in Him, but as more windows catch their attention, the greater their revelation will be, until the blessed day they accept Jesus as their savior. And on that day, the true beauty of their life, the unique masterpiece handcrafted by God, will be revealed.

And they will see that it is so very, very good.

───※───

> *". . . all the days ordained for me were written in your book*
> *before one of them came to be."*
> Psalm 139:16b

PART FIVE

Shop Till You Drop

Obvious

Jan Ackerson

Mrs. Keller is the best teacher! Last Monday she gave my Sociology class this awesome assignment to work on all week, and I know I'm going to ace it. It's the kind of thing I'm really good at.

So anyway, she tells us to spend the week observing people. How cool is that? Mrs. Keller said we can learn a lot about people just by watching them, and noticing things like their clothes and stuff.

And—get this—I work at Kroger's after school, so I spent the whole week figuring people out, just by the groceries they bought. Most of them just bought regular stuff—you know, like cereal and toilet paper—but I had some interesting ones, too, and those are the people I'm going to write my report about.

This one old lady came in, and she bought like a ton of cat food. Her clothes were so totally thrift shop grandma. She bought some old lady food, too, like white bread and tea. So I figure she's one of those crazy cat ladies who has a dozen cats crawling all over the place.

Wilma Longacre neatly arranged twenty cans of cat food—one week's supply—on the bottom shelf of a kitchen cabinet. With stiff fingers she used a can opener on the twenty-first can, and spooned its contents into a flowery china saucer, chipped in two places. When the teakettle whistled, she steeped a new teabag in a cup of steaming water, then saved it for tomorrow in a little bowl. One dainty bite at a time, she spooned a bit of cat food onto a slice of bread, eating a solitary meal in a silent kitchen.

Then there was this guy who had his shopping cart full of all these fancy foods. They were all *ingredients*, like stuff you'd see on the Food Network. You know, like fresh rosemary and prosciutto from the deli and pine nuts—all this *lah-dee-dah*, and it cost him a couple hundred bucks. He didn't have a wedding ring, and he was dressed really nice, so I'm thinking he's a "lifelong bachelor", *if* you know what I mean, and a gourmet cook. That's a no-brainer.

"What was I thinking?" Jason surveyed his kitchen in utter dismay. The walls were splattered with oozing lumps, several pots had overflowed, and smoke was pouring from the oven. He turned as his girlfriend appeared in the doorway, her eyes wide.

"This was supposed to be a romantic dinner, Katie." Jason cleared his throat and gestured grandly at the ruined kitchen. "This mess is like my heart before I met you," he ad-libbed. "But now I'm . . . like neater. Oh, crud, I'm messing this up." He took a deep breath. "Will you marry me?"

Okay, so then this mom came through my line, looking all stressed. She was buying M&M's® and Kool-Aid, junk like that. She wasn't that old, but she didn't do a thing to make herself look nice. It's too bad because she could have been really cute, for a mom. I bet she feeds her kids junk to get them to be quiet while she watches soap operas.

Linda Howard grasped her son's hands to stop their flapping. Distressed at his captivity, Adam rocked back and forth, moaning. Linda sat next to him and bent her head to his level.

"Look at me, Adam. It's time to work on your pronouns."

"Work on your pronouns," Adam echoed, his voice toneless and low.

"Do you want candy, Adam?"

"You want candy?" He freed his hands and flapped.

"No, say, 'I want candy,' Adam." Linda held out one of the M&M's®.

Adam reached for the chocolate. "I want candy, Adam."

Linda sighed and tried again.

And I've saved the best for last. This young guy came in, and I knew him, a little bit. All he bought was a twelve-pack of beer, but here's the deal—he graduated a few years ago, with my sister, and I happen to know that he's this super-religious youth pastor or something like that. So I concluded that Mr. Christian is nothing but a big old hypocrite.

Zach sat on the porch step next to his brother, setting the beer between them. "So, bro—I'm taking you up on it."

Trent looked skeptical. "What's this?"

"You said you'd let me talk to you about God when we could talk together over a cold brewski. So—you listening?"

I think Mrs. Keller is going to be really impressed with my project. I'll type it up with a fancy font and put it in one of those folders for holding reports. I've noticed that she always gives extra credit for that.

Like I said, I'm great at observing people. They're all pretty obvious, don't you think?

Shortage Economy

JOE HODSON

THE RUSSIAN SKIES HAD run out of sunshine. Gray clouds left the town a colorless painting of salt-stained sidewalks and long waiting lines. Gusts of wind punched through the row of brick houses and shops in the town square, shaking the awnings and shutters.

Mama's eyes were bleary, the way they get when she says she's not tired. Strands of black hair poked out from the scarf around her head, touching her face. I clung to the security of her hand as we waited in another line outside the grocery store. This time, it ran all the way past the edge of the block, almost to the place where Mama sometimes buys fabric to make quilts.

My legs hurt and I was cold. I grew fidgety.

"Katya," Mama snapped.

I stopped. Her face was stern; she was not in the mood for my restlessness.

Somewhere in front of us (I was too little to see where) I heard voices whispering about the government. I bent my head toward the sound of conversation and caught familiar words: *shortage* and *Brezhnev*. The wind scattered the rest of the conversation high into the bare trees.

Brezhnev. Papa and Mama would sometimes say that name in the house after dinner when they drank tea and had grown-up talk. Mama told me that he ran the country, but whenever I'd ask Papa, he'd laugh and tell me, "Oh, Katya, you're too young to worry about politics. Russia takes good care of us."

We needed toilet paper. So did everyone else. The stores ran out a week ago. Last time we came, Mama was able to buy extra and make it last. Papa has a friend he plays cards with who manages the grocery store. Sometimes he tells us when he thinks things might run out.

Papa's friend didn't know about the bread, though. We needed bread for dinner. Hopefully there would still be some left.

Here, grown-ups cry sometimes like children do. Once, Mama cried, too, when there was no more bread. She hid her face in her hands. I cried so she would stop. She pulled one of Papa's handkerchiefs from her purse and bent down and wiped my cheeks. "I'm sorry, Katya," she told me. "I didn't mean to frighten you. I stopped crying. See?"

In the line, Mama and I were closed in by bodies on both sides. We were a link in an endless chain. My mind floated somewhere else. Everyone was wearing fur coats, and for a while I pretended they were hungry bears growling at each other instead of talking.

A grey-bearded man standing behind us wore a warm hat cocked to one side. I looked up at him and my eyes traced the wrinkles in his face like a maze, following them up to the deeper ones by his eyes. This game went on until he noticed me and smiled. I hid behind my mother's legs, peeking at him from under her coat.

When we got to the storefront, the line fed into a room of empty faces. Papa's friend was helping keep wait-weary people from pushing ahead in line. "Yegor!" Mama shouted to him over the people's heads. "Is there bread?"

"Sorry, Lyubov," he replied.

Inside the grocery store, children cried to go home while adults argued over the last of things. Many of the shelves were bare, exposing the blank wall behind them. Condiments and pet food sat in heaps, untouched, as did other untouched goods. Another line, reaching the back of the store, was for those waiting at the cash register.

There were no apples for applesauce, but there was plenty of baby food. Mama put two jars in her grocery bag. They would have to do. A small sack of potatoes sat alone on a shelf. Something we could trade to a neighbor for bread. Mama grabbed it, a light hum coming from her lips. I recognized it. It was the Psalm Mama sings to me when I wake up at night afraid of the dark.

I sang the words I knew so well:

> "Surely goodness and mercy shall follow me
> All the days of my life, all the days of my life;
> And I will dwell in the house of the Lord
> Forever, forever, forever, Amen." [1]

Mama stopped and knelt down to my level. "I love you, Katya."
I felt her warm tears when she hugged me. But I was not frightened.

---

[1] Psalm 23:6

Manna Hills Mercantile

MYRNA NOYES

*T*HE BELL JINGLE-JANGLED merrily as I pushed open the wooden door of Manna Hills Mercantile. It was as if I'd stepped back a century to the time of my grandmother's childhood. The long, narrow building had a well-worn and rather creaky wooden floor, with old-time glass display cases lining one side of the wide center aisle. Wooden shelves stocked with canned and boxed goods ran the length of the room on both walls. Opposite the glass cases were bins overflowing with produce, and along the back wall stood a more modern-looking refrigerated section and a large freezer chest. A double row of bare light bulbs hung from the high ceiling at even intervals on either side of the aisle way.

I was gazing about in delight when from behind a glass case arose a grinning, gnome-like older man in a white apron. "Be with you in a minute, miss, soon as I finish rearranging these things. Shopping baskets are there by the door." He bent down, disappearing once more.

Looking where he'd pointed, I saw several sturdy, woven hand baskets stacked in a neat pile on the floor. Again, I had an odd impression of having stumbled through a portal into a past dimension, and I briefly considered hurrying back outside to the "real" world. I brushed that thought aside, however, and grabbed a basket, deciding to look around a bit.

Hmmm, the prices aren't old-fashioned, I mused. *$5.98 per pound for grapes certainly isn't what great-grandma paid.*

I walked nearer, and my nose wrinkled upon inspection of the smelly, moldy fruit. "These don't look good at all!"

"That's a fact, miss; they sure don't," interjected a genial voice. "These never look good, and they taste even worse, setting people's teeth on edge."

Startled, I whirled around to see the little storekeeper, who'd come up behind me unnoticed. "Then why do you sell them?" I blurted.

"Well, now, these are called grapes of wrath, and some people like to use them because their grandparents and parents did. They make a bitter wine from them that sours the stomach and stunts the soul."

I made a mental note; this guy was strange.

"I can see you don't like them; however, I think you might be interested in these fruits of the Spirit over here. They contain natural sugar which sweetens and refreshes not only the mouth and stomach but also the heart."

He held up a shiny, red fruit somewhat resembling an apple. "You don't find this variety in most stores nowadays. It's an heirloom called Charity. Here, smell and feel it yourself."

As I grasped it, a pleasant, warm, somewhat tingly sensation spread up through my fingers to my chest. *What's going on here?*

Next, he motioned toward some other unfamiliar fruits: "These are Joy, Peace, and Faith."

"Uh, thanks for your help," I mumbled, plunking a few of the fruits in my basket and moving on down the aisle. *This is getting weirder by the second.*

I passed by the "junk food" section, grinning at some of the labels I glimpsed—Couch-potato Chips, Prune-face Danish, Pickle-puss Relish, Sour-grapes Candy. *Maybe I'm having a kooky dream.*

Near the aisle's end, I noticed several bins holding bulk nuts, grains, and cereals. One was labeled "Wild Oats," and as I peered into it, the storekeeper's voice made me jump again.

"These wild oats never cook up the way you think they will," he warned amiably. "They're poor quality, not processed carefully, and may contain bits of rock and other foreign matter. People want them because they're cheap."

"Ugh," I replied, moving toward the refrigerated section. There I found crystal-clear bottled Water of Life and two brands of milk: Milk of Human Kindness and Pure Spiritual Milk. I grabbed a case of water and began making my way back to the front of the store. As I went, I picked up some 100% Pure Oil of Gladness and an aromatic loaf of Bread of Life baked by the Heavenly Manna Company.

As I placed my items on the counter and opened my purse, the storekeeper handed me a scrap of paper. "Wait, miss. Here's a coupon."

My eyes widened as I read, "'All your items are available without money and without price.' You're not serious?"

"Oh, yes! You are a mighty discerning woman, as everything you chose is no charge."

Dumbfounded, I smiled my thanks and left.

As I drove away, I glanced back . . . but the store was nowhere to be seen.

It's So Easy

CASSIE MEMMER

It also forced all people . . . to receive a mark on their right hands
or on their foreheads, so that they could not buy or sell
unless they had the mark, which is the name of the beast
or the number of its name.
Revelation 13:16-17

AT THE SOUND OF her daughter's cry, Marian wrapped her sweater tighter around her shoulders and hurried to the crib. Picking up the toddler, she murmured sweet words of comfort to the hungry girl. Lanie cried harder.

"I'm sorry, sweetie. I know you're hungry. I haven't been able to buy groceries for weeks. Daddy's out trying, but every place turns him away. Hopefully, today he'll find someone willing to help us. Here, let Mama rock you. That'll make you feel better, won't it?"

Marian threw a heavy comforter over herself and the child on her bosom. After a few moments, Lanie's cries changed to whimpers, but silent tears rolled down the cheeks of her grieving mother. *It's been days since we've eaten or had any decent water. How long have we been without heat and electricity?*

"God, if you're out there, what are we to do? We can't go on like this. We have money in the bank that we can't use. Jobs to go to, if only—"

A knock at the door interrupted her prayer. Fear wrenched Marian's stomach, until she heard her friend's voice. "Marian? You home?"

"Come on in, Joyce."

"Hey, girlfriend." Joyce strolled in and flopped down on the couch. "How's things going?"

"About the same." She waved an arm about the chilly room. "What have you been up to?"

"Just got back from shopping the new way. It's so easy. Walk into any store, pick up what you want, scan each item as you put it in the cart, and out the door you go. No checks, no cash, no cards." Joyce reached into her bag. "Hey, I sneaked you a can of soup, but don't tell anyone. They're keeping a close eye on how much everyone's buying. They're trying to track down everyone like you and Paul; trying to persuade everyone to join the program."

"Thank you! I'll give some of this to Lanie right now."

They moved to the kitchen and Marian used a manual can opener to open the soup. "She'll have to eat this cold. We've not had electricity for a week now."

She carefully fed Lanie, making sure not to lose one drop of the precious soup. The toddler didn't seem to care that the soup was cold. She gobbled it down.

"Eat some yourself, Marian."

"No, I'll save the rest for Paul," she said, her mouth watering. "He'll be home soon. He's been out since morning looking for help."

"How long are you going to go on like this? It could be so easy for you. You could have access to your bank accounts; Paul could go back to his old job. All you have to do is get the mark. What's the big deal? It makes everything easier. They would give you back your utilities, and you could shop for all you need, every day if you wanted. I'm telling you, it's painless."

Joyce laid her hand on the table. "Look, see? It's not that big, not that noticeable, and you'd never have to listen to Lanie cry again because of hunger. What's keeping you from doing what the government wants you to do? Everyone's doing it. It's the way of the future. Come on, while Lanie's content, I'll drive you down to the station where they're giving the marks. Then I'll take you straight to the grocery store. Okay?"

Marian hesitated. "Paul remembers hearing his grandmother talk about a time like this. She told him to never take the mark. Said to do so would betray God."

"But look at you, Marian. What has God done for you? You sit here watching your baby starve. You're being an unfit mother. They'll take Lanie away from you."

Yes, where have you been, God? Do you even exist? Marian felt nauseous. "Perhaps getting the mark is what I need to do, whether Paul does or not. At least one of us could access our funds and shop. And then he wouldn't have to go against his grandmother's advice."

Resolutely, Marian stood up from the table. "I've made my decision. Joyce. I accept your offer. Let's go to the marking station . . . then let's go shopping."

"Honey, I'm home. Great news! I found us some help. I've found some underground Christians. They know what we need to do to survive this madness taking over the world . . .

"Marian? Honey?"

The Shopping Rhino

WILLIAM PRICE

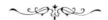

SITTING AT HIS DESK, Wilson Goldberg ate half of a peanut butter and jelly sandwich. He had the satisfied look of one eating the finest caviar. The businessman sighed as the alarm on his old wristwatch interrupted his meal. "One o'clock; lunchtime is over." He silenced the alarm and placed the uneaten half sandwich on top of the opened Bible he had been reading.

Wilson's office was in the rear of his jewelry store, and he was about to make his way to the storefront when his clerk's voice screeched over the intercom.

"Mr. Goldberg, you better get out here quick."

"I'm coming, Robin. Is everything okay?"

"You just need to get out here, boss."

Wilson quickly marched toward the lobby of his store where Robin stood pointing at the front door. He turned his gaze to the entrance. A grin slowly crept across his face as a tear formed in his right eye.

"Mr. Goldberg! What are you smiling at? Can't you see there's a rhinoceros at the front door."

Wilson's voice was calm and clear. "Robin, you didn't call anybody, did you?"

"No, sir, I was kind of freaked out."

"Good. Stand back, please."

"Mr. Goldberg, what do you think you're doing?"

Wilson walked to the entrance, where he slowly opened the double glass doors and allowed the rhino to enter. There was a crowd of people standing across the street. Wilson waved at them before closing the front doors.

Once inside, the rhinoceros tilted its large horn and nose up in the air. Robin jumped up on the counter next to the cash register. "Mr. Goldberg, I think we need to contact somebody."

"Don't worry, Robin; it's not here to hurt anyone."

The gray beast made its way to the back of the store, where the one-ton herbivore slowly bulldozed through Wilson's office door, ripping the frame from the wall.

At Wilson's desk, the rhino incredibly ate the half sandwich off the Bible. "Amazing. God, You're awesome." Wilson smiled.

When the rhino was finished eating, it turned around and walked back out into the storefront, where Robin hid behind the four policemen she had let in.

"Mr. Goldberg," spoke an officer with sergeant stripes on his shirtsleeve, "you need to stay away from the animal. It wandered from a zoo transport vehicle involved in an accident down the street. It might be disorientated. Zoo officials are coming."

"I'm not afraid, officer. This rhino isn't lost. It's shopping for my wife."

The sergeant looked confused. Robin whispered in his ear, "Mr. Wilson's wife died a year ago. He hasn't been quite right since."

The beast began moving from one showcase to the other, stopping at the wristwatch display. With one effortless thrust of its horn, the rhino broke the glass. When the animal turned back toward Wilson, a gold watch hung on the end of its horn.

"Mr. Goldberg, you may want to stand away." The sergeant unsnapped his gun holster.

The rhino and Wilson approached each other and stopped. The widower slowly reached out and removed the watch from the shopper's horn. He held the diamond-studded gold piece of jewelry against his heart.

"Pauline had wanted to buy me this very watch a year ago for our twenty-fourth," he said to the beast. "Did you know, on our very first anniversary, all we could afford to eat was peanut butter and jelly sandwiches?"

Wilson thought he saw the rhino wink its left eye as it turned and started to walk toward the front doors. The officers gave it a wide berth.

Outside, zookeepers had arrived with a large transport vehicle. The rhino walked up the ramp and disappeared into the darkness of its interior.

"Are you going to be all right, Mr. Goldberg?" the sergeant asked.

"Oh yes, sir. Did you know my wife had collected porcelain animal figures? I was going to buy her a hand-painted rhinoceros, but she died in a car accident before I had the chance."

～ঞ্জ৶～

After everyone cleared out of the store, Wilson locked the front doors and watched the zookeepers drive away. When he returned to his office, the alarm on his new timepiece began to beep. He looked at it and smiled. It was two o'clock, the same hour he and Pauline were married twenty-five years before.

Wilson refocused his attention to his jam-stained Bible.

Surely, death has been swallowed with victory and my sorrow for today has been turned to joy.

At the Dream Store

Holly Jensen

———⁓≈⊱✦⊰≈⁓———

I HAD COME TO THE dream store in search of a new dream. All those I had previously bought had been fulfilled. I had a family, a career, a nice house, and plenty of friends. One might wonder what more I could want, but I needed another goal for which I could strive; a dream I had not yet followed.

I searched through the shelves of dreams packed in cases designed to catch the seeker's interest. There were dreams of hilltop mansions, rising to fame and power, being beautiful, being wise, and so many more. None of these were what I wanted. I was happy with my house, my looks, with everything, but there was something missing, and I had come here looking for the answer.

Feeling frustrated and discouraged, I walked toward the exit.

The storeowner asked, "Did you find your dream today?"

"No," I answered, shrugging as though it didn't matter.

"Well, perhaps I can help. What sort of dream do you wish to follow?"

"That's the trouble! I don't exactly know. I want a dream that's special—one that won't be easy to follow, but will be rewarding. I want a dream that will last longer than I will."

"Ah," the man answered, "I have just the dream you want."

I followed him to the back of the shop and through a door I hadn't previously noticed.

"This is where our most priceless and difficult dreams are kept."

He reached up to a shelf that held a number of strange cross-shaped cases.

"Here," he said, handing me the case. "This is our most priceless dream."

It looked rather plain except for what appeared to be a red stain that ran down the length of the cross. I opened the case slowly. There was something about it that inspired the utmost reverence and care. Inside was the picture of a face, and although it smiled, I got the impression that it could be stern, too. The eyes were what struck me most—there was such a look of love in them.

There was something else as well. I felt as though whoever this was wanted to pull me apart and put me back together again in a different shape. Yet there was a promise in the look which seemed to say that once I was put back together again, something far better would be the result.

"What dream is this?" I asked.

"It is the dream of a personal relationship with that man. His name is Jesus Christ. When cared for properly, this dream will last forever without fading. It is also the dream that you will go to Heaven and live with Him when you die. In this lifetime, it will change you and make you better."

"How much does it cost?"

"Nothing down and zero payments."

Seeing my look of disbelief, he continued. "See that red stain on the case? Jesus died to pay for this dream. Yet it does cost in the end. This dream changes you. You will become more and more caught up in following it. People won't understand. Even your family may not understand. But there are those who will understand and join you in following this dream. In fact, there is a place where people gather to talk about how they may better follow it. If you decide you want to go on this journey, I will give you directions. There is also a guidebook that comes with the case."

I stared at the face of Jesus for a long time. The look in His eyes was drawing me, calling me with the promise of adventure. I knew, somehow, that this was what I'd been missing; this was the thing I had come to the dream store to find. The thought of what it could cost frightened me a little, but His face and the thought of what I would gain made my decision.

"I'll take it," I said.

He smiled and took a large book down from another shelf. Together we went to the front of the store where he wrapped the case and book in tissue paper and gave me a receipt.

In crimson letters it said: *Paid in full.*

Bruno's Shopping Junket

BETH LABUFF

Late summer, Monday, mid-July,
Year: Nineteen sixty-two,
An unlatched gate, an oversight,
Outcome: hullabaloo.

Brawny Bruno, Angus bull,
Escaped and seized the day.
Gate left dangling, no more wrangling,
From pastureland he strayed.

Bruno snorted, freedom sensed,
Belied mad-cow disease.
Bovine breakout from confinement,
Spurred by summer's breeze.

Westward on toward Chesterton,
An unsuspecting village.
Bruno trotted, head held high,
With cloven hooves to pillage.

'Round about noon, same summer day,
Old Bruno spied a door,
'Twas Grady's Mart on Maple Street
The town's lone grocery store.

Into this shop he horned his way,
Shoved customers aside,
Proceeded past the canned goods aisle,
The grocer he defied.

Through the produce Bruno roamed,
Ingested apples ripe.
Purloined carrots, beets, and kale
Digested in his tripe.

Shelves of bakery goods were tossed,
Relieved of cakes and pies.
Pastries trampled under hoof—
A bakery aisle demise.

Then to the chips and soda pop,
Without a backward glance,
Bruno bebopped through the snacks,
A bullish market dance.

His shopping frenzy trashed the place.
Left food strewn 'cross the floor,
Noodles, crackers, maple syrup,
"Clean-up on aisle four."

What currency did Bruno use,
For this, his luncheon bender?
The last I heard in this fair land,
Cow pies weren't legal tender.

"Eye for an eye," must be repaid,
So says the Holy Book,
The bull's infraction was a sin,
Bruno was ruled a crook,

The grocer uttered not a word,
Nor questions did he ask.
A minor scuffle could be heard,
One swiftly ended task.

New signs were posted on the wall,
Alas, here ends his tail.
"Brisket, Roasts—2.99"
Old Bruno was on sale!

~⚜~

"Breach for breach, eye for eye, tooth for tooth:
as he hath caused a blemish in a man,
so shall it be done to him again."
Leviticus 24:20 (KJV)

Felicity's Wonderful World

Helen Paynter

THE SUN WAS SHINING and the world was a wonderful place. Felicity smiled at herself in the plate glass window of the shop. Her reflection, all Calvin Klein and Gucci, smiled back.

And why shouldn't she smile? She was young, beautiful, and Daddy had lent her his credit card.

Turning into a clothing store, she began to examine the silk blouses, fingering the fabric with her lip curled, just as Mummy had taught her.

Jayani yawned and stretched. It had been a long shift, and she was looking forward to getting out. She couldn't tell the time, but she was listening for the buzzer that would signal her freedom.

Her supervisor walked over, frowning. "This work is below standard, Jayani. Look at these seams!"

Jayani flushed. "I'm very sorry, Mrs. Bassa. The baby was sick last night, and I had to help Mother take care of him. I'll try harder tomorrow."

Her superior shook her head, her lips pinched. "No you won't, young lady. You'll do them again before you leave. Here!" She dumped twenty silk blouses onto Jayani's table and hurried away.

With a sigh, Jayani took the top blouse from the pile. Screwing up her eyes in the fading light, she began to unpick the tiny stitches. It would be another four hours before the twelve-year-old made her way home.

Swinging her bag lightly from one finger, Felicity bounced onwards to the next store. She wanted to buy some jeans. Low waist, boot cut, understated but elegant. She knew just the place.

Kayin had finished work for the day. He stretched out his long legs and took thirsty gulps of the drink his wife had offered. In the evening shade, he sat outside his hut and gazed in sleepy contentment at his cotton crop.

For three days he had paced up and down every row, spraying the budding plants with the magic pesticide. He didn't know what it was, but it certainly worked. He'd watched earthworms shrivel and die before his eyes.

A sudden commotion. Two of his children tottered around the corner, carrying something between them. A cold hand grabbed Kayin's stomach and squeezed. "Adisa, Folami. What is it?"

"It's Oni, Father. We were playing in the shed. Where you keep the barrels."

"We don't know how it happened." Their naïveté was so evident in their voices; as yet they feared only a rebuke.

"She fell into the barrel, Father. The one that was half-full."

For every hour of the next two days, Kayin knelt beside the toddler's bed and prayed for her to die.

Felicity had several parcels now, and she was reaching the limit of her tolerance. Shop 'til you drop is an over-rated idea, she thought. After all, there's always tomorrow.

Just one more thing, then she would go home for a long, hot bath. But first, she needed cocoa butter skin cream—Mummy's beauty secret.

Kwame leaned down and gently disengaged his daughter's clinging fingers. "I have to go now, Efia."

The little girl looked up with sulky eyes. "I don't want you to go, Daddy. I want you to stay here with Mummy and me."

Kwame looked down at her, and across at his wife. Her grave eyes gazed back. She didn't understand either. Didn't or wouldn't. But how could he explain to them? The evidence was clear in their eyes—a good crop this year; the plants heavy with cocoa beans. How could he explain that he would be selling them at a loss? He understood little enough about it himself. All he knew was The Company had cut the prices again. All his wife knew was that her husband was leaving her with a child and another on the way.

"It's only for a while," he tried to reason. "I'll go and try my luck in the city; send some money home. And Yoofi will look after you." He ignored the frisson of fear that tickled his spine as he said this. His brother would never harm them.

"Come on, cheer up. When I come back I'll bring you a present." He grinned emptily, kissed his wife once more, ruffled Efia's hair, and turned away. With luck he'd catch a lift when he got to the main road.

When he returned a year later, he gave his wife AIDS.

Felicity stowed her bags carefully in the back of her sports car and spun homeward. The sun was shining and the world was a wonderful place.

Consider the Lilies of the Field

Loren T. Lowery

On a small swell of land just to the south of our house, set back and between a sixty-foot vine maple on one end and a twenty-foot hazelnut tree on the other, lives a nest of twelve wild sword ferns. On this fence-encircled knoll, with a pear tree grove to its west and horse pasture to its east, another world exists peacefully without markets, shops, or vendors. Currency is not needed here, nor would it ever be understood.

Trampled grass is its road, wild blackberries its harvest. Red mulberries spike it with color and gladden the sweep of winging birds. God is present here, in this fern grove—this Gilead. It is a wayside cathedral, set apart for those who by fate or happenstance step across its threshold.

The play of passive light, the moisture held in the air by the wavering ferns, the deep, fragrant smell of earth, the gentle embrace of silence is felt as the plants all seem to hold the world at bay outside its fenced barrier.

This plot of land is remarkable no matter the season or time of day. But mornings are my most treasured moments here, before chores and horses and other demands reach out to grab me.

In the pre-dawn light, the red vine maple stands as a dark silhouette against the morning sky, her willowy branches stretching upward like the graceful arms of a ballerina dancing to *Swan Lake*, but instead of white garland at the tips of her outstretched hands, it is crimson leaves, summer's first surrender to fall.

Here before day's onset, I make a chair of an alder stump. It is quiet and peaceful with the morning dew cooling the air. Possibly as Thoreau at Walden's Pond, I look around to see the sun touching our apple orchard, its warm kiss blushing the fruit-laden limbs now bent in autumn's haze to the ground. Bejeweled arms show off their finest gems of topaz, ruby, garnet, peridot, and emerald.

Closer still, within reach through the fenced barrier to the east, the pear trees have hung their succulent fruit like droplets of gold. To my right, the rich, earthly smell of wild geraniums scents the air. Beside me, the mulberry bush is bright with red berries, and to my left, the filbert tree, now lush with fall's new growth, fails to hide her bounty of clustered hazelnuts beneath vibrant, green leaves.

Birds of many varieties flit through the brushwood and undergrowth. Pelted animals burrow beneath the ground or hide in the hollows of tree and shrub. Insects scurry, buzz, and vainly attempt to secret themselves. Each creature called to sing and lend its voice, traveling the boundaries of the sanctuary with glad tidings, all lifting their voices as joyfully as carolers at Christmas time.

Here I am, clothed with the fabric of solitude and fed by the bounty of beauty. My thirst is quenched by the streams of color flowing from the rising and setting sun. I breathe the air of ancient forests, entertained by the choir of nature's voice, and I am comforted by the embrace of God's peace.

Merchants? Shopping? Currency? It is not needed here; nor would it ever be understood.

Rich

TAMMY BOVEE

A COLD, BLUSTERY WIND WHISTLED around the house. It echoed the emptiness I felt in my heart when I found Wiggles, my pet goldfish, floating dead in the hospital tank I had set up.

I wept as I called for my husband, Jeff. I had tried to help Wiggles, but he had been sick a long time. His sickness, and my inability to help him, hurt me deeply, reminding me of my inability to do anything to help with our financial reversals.

Soon Jeff was out for the shovel. He came back inside and placed his hand over the container where Wiggles' plump, lifeless body lay in a puddle. With bowed head he prayed, "Thank you God for the gift of Wiggles' life and the joy he gave to us while he was alive."

Jeff proceeded to bury the pet somewhere in the yard. "Deep enough so the neighborhood cats won't get it," I specified.

The solemn deed done, Jeff looked me in the eye and said, "Want to go get another goldfish?"

"But we don't have much money," I frowned. His paycheck was two weeks late and we were scrounging. But the look in Jeff's eye convinced me.

Pretty soon he was driving me down icy streets with our pet boxer, Fritzi, on my lap, trying to get to the pet store before it closed. We made it with a few minutes to spare.

I walked slowly over to the aquariums. The high-school aged clerk was already mopping the floors.

"Excuse me," I said, "could I still get a fish?"

"Sure," said the girl. Her ponytail swished as she put the mop aside.

"I'm replacing a fish that I just lost."

Patiently, she let me pick out a healthy little fish that looked a bit like a miniature Wiggles.

Fritzi entertained the pet store worker and another lady who had snuck into the store for a last minute purchase. Then Jeff and I headed back home.

As we settled in for the evening, we read our marriage devotional book. It talked about the importance of making deposits in each other's love accounts. I realized that was what Jeff had done for me. My new pet may only be small, but it meant so much to me.

I thanked my husband for Cal (my new goldfish), and realized once again that no matter what our financial picture, I was really a rich woman.

PART SIX

Putting Pen to Paper

The Runaway Writer

Kenn Allan

The day has come for me to write
The novel in my mind;
A thousand plots spin through my head
(Though none have been outlined).

With confidence, I grab my pen
And lock the office door,
Encouraged by the how-to books
I'd skimmed the night before.

A ream of paper on my desk
Lies waiting, clean and white,
Then, almost like a living thing,
My pen begins to write . . .

Upon a dark and stormy night
Beside a nameless sea,
A Hero treads upon the sand
For reasons known to he.

When suddenly a scream is heard
From somewhere up the beach;
The Hero sprints with nostrils flared
And brawn none dare impeach.

A Girl is fighting for her life
Against a dozen foes;
But thrashed by blazing martial arts
They flee The Hero's blows.

The Girl and Hero fall in love,
A most contentious pair—
Exchanging banter on the beach
To show how much they care.

In the meantime, far up north,
An earthquake shakes the Pole,
When sunlight heats the ozone shield
And thaws a gaping hole.

A pirate ship with frozen crew
Glides from its icy tomb,
Defrosted with a vengeful dream
That carnage should resume.

Perched atop a tidal wave
Caused by the polar quake,
It sails a Caribbean course,
With ice cubes in its wake.

Meanwhile, back upon the beach,
With lipstick smeared and kissed,
The Girl observes an attaché
Chained to The Hero's wrist.

She queries about what's inside;
His answer is concise:
The case contains a prototype—
A nuclear device.

No sooner was his secret spilled,
The ocean's surface cringes
And vomits forth a tidal wave
With ice-encrusted fringes.

It lifts The Hero off the shore
Amid cruel pirate laughter,
And slams him on a rotting deck—
The Girl came tumbling after.

Oh, what a valiant fight ensues
As rusty sabers clash,
But not one pirate hits the deck
Beneath The Hero's slash.

As chunks of epidermis fly,
One pirate loses face;
These aren't buccaneers at all . . .
But aliens from space!

They stun The Hero and the Girl
And share these fearsome facts:
They plan to microwave the earth
And use mankind as snacks.

The Girl attempts reciting poems
To woo the skinless crew,
But both were banished off the ship
By vote of 8-2.

The Hero drops his attaché
And flips a switch marked, "FIRE!"
Which starts them guessing which to cut:
The green or yellow wire?

He plops the Girl into a boat,
And drops both to the sea,
Then dives with pure Olympic grace
Near where she floated free.

Soon after climbing safe inside
And straining at the oars,
The Hero spies some dorsal fins
Of hungry dinosaurs.

Luckily, before they gnaw
The dinghy to a raft,
Some shots ring out from guns aboard
A naval landing craft.

Hooray! The soldiers save the day!
But each one fears his fate,
And shares sad tales of hometown bliss
Before it is too late.

The Hero comforts one and all
With super-sized conviction,
Reciting Scripture just enough
To deem this Christian fiction.

Then with a loud unnerving jolt
The transport runs aground,
And soldiers spill onto the beach
While bullets whiz around.

A sergeant taps The Hero's arm,
With helmet in his hand,
And begs for him to lead the troops
To free this troubled land.

Up the hill the soldiers charge
Where angels fear to tread,
To face an enemy from hell—
An army of the dead!

Their evil leader spurs them on;
A wizard dressed in black,
Who casts his spells with deadly aim
Astride a dragon's back.

One of these curses hits the beach
And zaps the Girl in hiding
Who turns into an octopus
With tentacles a-sliding.

Then suddenly, a mushroom cloud
Glows in the distant sky,
And airborne bits of pirate ship
Rain down in great supply.

Like a spear, the mizzen mast
Impales the wizard's chest;
His body crumbles into dust
Along with troops possessed.

But sadly, at the water's edge,
The victory is flawed—
The Hero learns the Girl he loves
Remains a cephalopod.

Reflecting on their moments shared,
And kids not meant to be,
Our Hero rips free from her hugs,
And lobs her out to sea.

I scrawl *The End* and sheath my pen,
Exhausted without equal . . .
Perhaps I'll take a little nap
Before I write the sequel.

Unwritten

LORI OTHOUSE

*T*HE INSTRUMENT PAUSED TENTATIVELY over the blank page, the last page. Trembling fingers clutched it tightly, as if afraid to let go. It was the final chapter in a story with great potential, but seemingly destined to a tragic ending. Disappointment had crept in, along with its lethal partner, doubt, and now only waited to see the fruit of its labors . . . the book would be closed forever.

Sydney tugged at the unlabeled box crammed into the corner of the garage. Nothing.

She took a deep breath, tightened her grip and yanked again. Suddenly it gave way, sending her backward and landing squarely on her lap. She groaned, slowly stood, and resolved once again not to put off spring cleaning for so long.

She carried the box inside and plopped it on the kitchen table. Expecting old clothes or books, she stopped short upon seeing the contents. A large portfolio sat on top of numerous notebooks, writing magazines, and textbooks. Hesitantly, she pulled out the heavy binder and opened it for the first time in years.

Inside the front cover was a quote from a college professor: *Your life is unwritten—make every word count.*

A rather outspoken Christian, his inspiration was infectious. The years seemed to rewind in a sweet haziness as she turned the pages. It was her dream once, this solitary, introverted life of a writer. But the smile from her first feeble attempts quickly turned to a frown when she observed the increasing number of red marks and comments on her work:

Flat.

Lifeless.

Where's the passion?

What did that mean? Writing *was* her passion . . . wasn't it? Even now, reading her professor's words was humiliating. As inspiring as he was, his criticism was crippling. Obviously, being a writer was not God's plan for her.

Not wanting to go there again, she quickly repacked the box, closed it and carried it outside. It dropped with a dull *thud* next to the garbage can.

Sydney turned to go back inside, not looking back.

Heavy drops of rain beat against the windowpane. Sydney heard them vaguely in the distance, but couldn't feel them. She walked along a narrow path, alone. A boisterous noise to her left caused her to look up. There were people, multitudes of them, walking in a wide-open area. They were laughing, talking, obviously having a good time and Sydney felt somewhat envious of them.

A flickering light ahead of them turned her gaze forward. Squinting at it, she caught her breath. There was a jagged cliff at the end of the path, with flames engulfing the great chasm below. She immediately knew them to be the flames of Hell. Looking back at the crowd, she realized in horror that they couldn't see their destination. They were walking right into eternal death and didn't even know it.

Instinctively, Sydney screamed for them to stop, but to no avail. Not one of them could hear her.

Desperate to help, she found a pen and paper and scribbled out a warning, clumsily throwing it toward the crowd. A few people stopped, picked up the paper and read it. Their eyes opened wide, spiritually as well as physically. They began to turn around and make their way toward her.

It worked! But there were still so many more out there. How could she possibly reach them all? Suddenly, she saw her former professor on the path with her.

"Look at them!" she cried desperately. "They can't hear me. I have to write to them, but it only reaches a few at a time."

Her professor smiled. "Congratulations, Sydney. You've finally found your passion. Now write."

With a loud clap of thunder, everything went black . . .

Instantly awake, Sydney sat up in bed, her heart racing. The realization of what she had seen began to sink in. Without hesitation or shoes, she bolted outside.

Her fingers dug into the soggy cardboard as she carefully brought her box back inside. Shivering with cold and anticipation, she slowly reopened the box, and her dream.

The instrument quickened in the now steady hand that held it. Hitting the page deliberately, it began the next chapter and found it wasn't the last, but the first of many yet to be written. Disappointment and doubt could not be found. There was no longer room for such indulgences. The ending of the story had changed.

Writing Maranda

JAN ACKERSON

*M*ARANDA COVERED HER FACE with her pale hands and wept bitterly, her golden tresses veiling her ivory arms. Her world had shattered forever with that knock at the door . . .

I paused at my computer, grinning. This was my first foray into the world of romance writing, and I was nailing it. My characters were practically writing themselves, and all I had to do was throw a few extra adjectives and adverbs into each paragraph.

Her porcelain cheeks stained with tears, Maranda grasped the photograph of Rodrigo that adorned her mahogany bedside table. "Oh, Rodrigo," she whispered quietly, clasping the silver frame to her flawless bosom—

I was startled by the doorbell. Muttering, I stomped to the hallway, wondering who dared interrupt me when the words were flowing so freely. A delivery truck idled in the driveway, and a man with a clipboard stood on my porch.

I yanked the door open, peeved by the interruption and anxious to get back to Maranda's weeping.

"Yes?"

The man looked down at his clipboard. "I got a delivery for Jennica Groves. That you?"

I wasn't expecting anything, but . . . "Yes, that's me."

He waved at the truck. There was a flurry of activity, then three men started toward the house, struggling under the weight of a square box no bigger than a microwave, but obviously very heavy. I opened the door and they dropped it on the living room floor with a thud.

"What is it?" I asked, the sound still reverberating.

"Writer's block, ma'am." The three helpers were panting and wiping their foreheads.

"Wha—a writer's block? I didn't order that! Take it back!"

"Sorry, lady, no can do. I just deliver 'em." He tipped his cap and the crew hustled away.

I turned and stared at the box. A writer's block—how ridiculous!

Kneeling to remove the packaging, I found that I couldn't budge the thing at all. It must have weighed several hundred pounds.

Well, who cares?

I left the block and returned to my computer.

Maranda's sapphire eyes filled . . .

Maranda's aching heart . . . ached . . .

It was hopeless. I had no idea what Maranda was going to do once she stopped crying. All I could think about was that block. Who sent it? How could I get rid of it?

For several days, I wrestled with the block. I tried to chip away at it and broke my only screwdriver. I bruised three toes kicking the thing. Having heard that cola would eat through anything, I poured an entire bottle on it.

Nothing happened.

Maranda twiddled her thumbs . . .

Maranda skipped about the room . . .

No use.

I couldn't write anything with that writer's block around. I decided to clean the house instead. I was dancing with the feather duster when I heard the doorbell chime. Now what? I peered through the curtains; a young woman stood on the landing, looking vaguely familiar. I opened the door.

"May I help you?"

"I'm Miranda. Can I come in?"

My life was getting stranger and stranger. But I had to admit that she certainly looked like Maranda. Golden tresses, porcelain skin . . .

"Um, sure."

She pushed past me and plopped onto a chair. "So, here's the deal," she said. "I don't like the way you've been writing me. First of all, you spelled my name wrong. It's M-I-R-A-N-D-A, okay?"

"But I—"

"Yeah, whatever." She waved a hand in the air. "And listen, how about giving me a better personality? Some spunk, maybe? I'm really tired of this weeping and sobbing routine, you know?"

"Uh, okay, I can do—"

Miranda leaned forward and patted my arm. "Listen, you're not a bad writer. You made me real beautiful—I like that. Just lay off all the damsel-in-distress stuff, okay?"

I nodded, still stunned to be conversing with my protagonist in my own living room.

She continued. "Just so you know—Rodrigo doesn't die. I think he does, and I let Pemberton comfort me, and then Rodrigo returns and I have to choose. Everyone thinks I'm going back to Rodrigo, but it turns out Pemberton is cooler after all. Got it?"

"Okay, but Rodrigo—"

Miranda snorted. "He's all tanned skin and flashing black eyes, but he's never had a deep thought in his life." She stood up, tossing her hair. "So—are we all set? I'll just be taking this, then."

With no effort, she lifted the writer's block to her shoulder and walked outside, pausing briefly to flash me a charming smile—her lips dewy, her teeth like pearls.

An Innocent Error of Joy

ANN GROVER

THEO SHIFTED THE HERB basket restlessly from hand to hand. Scents of sage and summer savory teased his nostrils, and a sneeze tightened behind his eyes.

"Theo, you'll upend the basket if you don't stop your fidgeting," Brother Phelan reprimanded softly as he plucked a few sprigs of vervain.

"I'm sorry, Brother Phelan." Theo watched in fascination as a caterpillar crawled along the friar's cowl and disappeared into a woolen fold.

"Come, Theo."

Theo followed the portly monk through the monastery garden, resisting the temptation to swing the basket against the greenery along the path. Phelan pushed against an oaken door, and they entered the aromatic room where he concocted healing tinctures and ointments. "Leave the herbs and find Father Libran."

Theo did as bidden, but not before stopping to watch a lark spiraling in its heavenward flight, its song pure and clear. Theo flung out his arms in imitation of the lark's soaring ascension, and he broke into a joyous run, not pausing until he reached Father Libran's quarters.

"Theo." Father Libran peered at Theo's sweaty face and disheveled tunic. "You must be still. Quiet yourself before God. Remember the writing brothers are working, and we must not disturb them."

Theo cast down his eyes. "Yes, Father."

"Now remove the ashes and bring firewood."

"Yes, Father."

At midday, Theo stood at the back of the chapel while the monks recited prayers. The resonating echoes in the stone hall uplifted him, but he was soon distracted by the flickering shadows dancing among the stone pillars.

After prayers, Brother Beathan approached Theo. One of the writing brothers!

"Come, Theo." The monk led the way to the scriptorium where the gospels were being penned in Latin.

Theo had been to the scriptorium once before and had caught a tiny glimpse of the brilliantly colored pages as he'd picked up feather parings from the floor.

Brother Crimthann and Brother Aindrias were already bent over their vellum pages, their quills quivering, the holy words coming alive in the illuminated drawings that were adorning the scriptures.

Theo approached the work bench and gazed in awe. How amazing! To be able to write, to read, to paint the glowing pictures that decorated the pages. Theo was lightheaded with the thought, and he feared the friars could hear his heart pulsating within his chest. He watched, enthralled, as the brothers stroked, dipped, stroked.

"Theo," Brother Beathan whispered, "please bury this old gall-ink. It is useless and must be returned to the earth. Theo?" He laid a stained hand on Theo's shoulder, a hint of a smile playing about his lips.

"Yes, Brother Beathan."

Reluctantly, Theo left the scriptorium.

But Theo could not stop thinking of the writing, the words, each smooth folio. It was mysterious, unfathomable, as holy and sacred as God Himself. Theo gave the sky a glance, as if God might be offended to be compared to soot marks on calfskin. But it was His hallowed Word after all, was it not?

After that, Theo was called to perform tasks in the scriptorium often, sweeping up spilled soot, scraping hardened egg yolk from the stone floor, fetching items, all under Brother Beathan's knowing eye. Theo's heart became more eager.

One night, Theo tossed on his pallet as images from the radiant pages beckoned to him—peacocks and lions, oxen and quail. Unable to withstand, he arose and tiptoed to the scriptorium, where pages from the day's work were drying, gleaming in the bright moonlight.

How glorious and splendid! Surely an angel had swept a wing across the calfskin and left a celestial signature. No mortal was capable of such artistry, such genius. Theo followed the intricate knotwork until he was dizzy.

And the script! The Word of God penned through the hand of man.

What possessed Theo to touch the quill? To dip it in the horn of gall-ink? He found where one of the brothers had left off in the middle of a word.

Dare he?

Holding the quill as he had seen the brothers do, he chose a simple letter from a line of text. He held his breath and carefully formed an "a." Theo's heart thudded in triumph and trepidation, but choosing another letter, he laboriously stroked a "u."

Theo collapsed in the moonlight, his soul enraptured.

In the morning, Brother Crimthann finished the word, and the verse read, "I came not only to send peace, but *joy*."

An error, yet a truth, nevertheless.

⁓⊱✵⊰⁓

Author's Note:

This is a fictitious accounting for an error written in the *Book of Kells*. In Matthew 10:34b, the Latin word for sword is "*gladium*," but in this version, the word for joy, "*gaudium*," was written instead.

Opa's Writer

HOLLY JENSEN

~·~·~

EVER SINCE THE AGE of six, I have lived with my grandparents. When I was twelve, Opa began losing his sight. By the time I was fourteen, it was almost gone. Not an easy thing to deal with in any case, but this was especially hard for Opa because he was a writer who was either too feeble or too stubborn to learn Braille.

I didn't know what to do to help him. He was not the smiling Opa of my early years who loved to laugh and sing, but a depressed shadow of himself.

One night as the three of us sat talking, he burst out, "This would not be so bad if I could still write!"

There was silence. We didn't know what to say. There was nothing to say. The shadow of Opa's growing darkness was spreading over all of us.

I went to bed and prayed for an hour. I asked God to help Opa, and to help us to help him, if He wished.

That night I had the strangest dream. Opa was completely blind, but he was writing. Stranger still, the hand holding the pen wasn't his hand at all. It wasn't big and work-worn, but small and young.

I said nothing about it the next morning, but I went to school praying that God would show me what it meant, if anything. During art class, as I was painting some clouds in a blue sky, a picture from the dream flashed across my mind. I almost dropped the paint brush when I realized it was my hand holding the pen.

I could be Opa's pen-holder. Would I do it, though? It would mean time and sacrifice. Opa was hard to stop, once he started writing. Deep inside, though, I knew it was God's answer to my prayer. I prayed that God would give me willingness, and then went home with an excited heart.

That night, I asked to talk to Opa. How would I start? Surely he wouldn't want my help. But I knew this was right, so I took a deep breath.

"Opa, I had a dream last night that you were writing."

"A dream is all that is left."

"No, Opa, it isn't. Your heart with God in it. That's what's left. You always told me that writing isn't something you do with a pen, but something God does with your heart. Now, you can't use a pen, but I can."

"You want to write for me, yes?"

"Yes, Opa," I answered, fully realizing the truth of it for the first time. "I do."

There was silence. I knew Opa was thinking on what I had said and that no more talk was needed. Finally he spoke.

"You would write *auf Deutsch* for me?"

"Of course I would."

"Well, *liebchen*, we may try."

Tears in my eyes, I hugged him then ran to fetch a pen and paper.

"Shall we start?" I asked.

Opa smiled and we began.

That night we spent three hours together, as God wrote with Opa's heart and my pen. I went to bed with more joy than I'd felt in a long time.

It was a new beginning for Opa, too. He was more like himself, laughing and singing old German hymns with us of an evening. He could still write. Compared to this, going blind was merely one of those trials to be dealt with in this life. I write everything for him, and Oma does it when I'm not there.

It is funny to see the looks of passersby when he says, "*Liebchen*, I need to write this down."

It is good to see their smiles when I pull a notebook out of my purse and he begins to dictate.

It was he who asked me to tell this story. He wants the world to know what God can do with willing hearts. Let God be your light and your pen, and the darkness can never take hold.

Dueling Solutions

WILLIAM PRICE

THE SMALL FLAT IS silent and dimly lit. The cursor blinks like a heartbeat on the empty word processing. Hunter Gates lights a cigarette as he considers the right words to type. A swirling cloud of exhaled smoke fogs the small room. A sweating glass of iced tea sits next to his computer on top of a black, leather-bound Bible. He slowly takes a drink and sets the tumbler back down.

At least it makes a good coaster.

On the other side of the laptop lies a 9mm revolver. His quivering right hand caresses the coolness of its blue steel. The irony of the props in front of him causes Hunter to cast a wry grin.

Only God could have scripted this scene. To my left, a Bible sits silent, never opened. To my right, a gun lies harmlessly still. A blank computer screen, symbolic of the answers I don't have to impossible questions, is sandwiched between the two solutions, neither of which I have much experience using.

Hunter's hands hover over the keyboard, waiting for direction, and then he starts to type.

> *Dear family,*
>
> *As I write this, I am faced with a great dilemma.*
>
> *As you know, I am in trouble. I appreciate all of your support and prayers, but I do not think I can spend the next twenty years in prison. I seriously doubt the jury will have mercy on me when my trial is over. I've spent every penny I had on my defense and on bond money to keep me out of jail—to this point. I have nothing left but the scalding reality of my actions.*
>
> *The only thing I've ever had in my life is writing. It was always so easy creating fictional characters, but now, as I write about myself, I struggle for the right words.*
>
> *I don't know how the story will end. I have no control over the plot. I can't delete words already written. They are facts now*

eternally printed. I got drunk, drove when I shouldn't have, and killed a mother. I know I deserve punishment. I'm not even sure at this point if I deserve to live.

It's not the prison time I fear; it's the guilt of living. I'll never forget the expressions on the woman's family in court. I know they hate me. But if truth be known, their hate for me is nothing compared to the hate I have for myself.

Even as I type this I do not know what I am going to do. I have a Bible to my left and a newly purchased pistol to my right. If you end up reading this you'll know I chose the right.

Hunter quits typing and gazes at the Bible under his iced tea.

God, if I give the gun here one chance, I know it'll work. So I'm going to open this Bible and see what it says. I'm not afraid to die. I'm not afraid to be punished. But I am afraid, and I don't know why.

Hunter removes the iced tea from the Bible and picks it up. He leafs through the pages and points his finger at a scripture.

After he reads it, he snaps the book closed, sets it down, and picks up the pistol. His finger trembles on the trigger.

He closes his eyes.

Then he opens one eye. He sees the cursor still blinking on the computer screen, waiting for more words. He lays the gun back down.

Okay, God, I'm a writer myself, and I know you can't judge a book by one sentence. So, I'm going to give it another chance. By the way, I already knew the punishment for sin was death, but there must be more to the story. I haven't even met your main character yet.

Hunter shuts off his computer, picks up the Bible and goes to bed, where he reads until he falls asleep.

~⚜~

Four weeks later, Hunter is writing another letter, but this one is with a pencil on paper.

Dear family,

Just want you all to know that I have chosen life. I'll explain what that means later, but I want to say I know Jesus loves me, though I still don't know why.

I am going to continue writing in prison. I'm working on a novel called Dueling Solutions. *I'm not sure how it's going to end yet, but I know God will help me find it.*

Memories of Miss Cochrane's Class

TERI WILSON

*H*OLLY LOOKED AT ALL the white bakers' bags hanging from the chalkboard at the front of the classroom. As usual, the bags belonging to the popular girls bulged and overflowed, straining to contain all the paper Valentine cards within.

Holly was not one of the popular girls. Her bag dangled limply from its place, the buff cocker spaniel she had drawn on the front staring back at her with big, sad eyes.

"Class, if your math assignment is complete you may come get your Valentine bag." Miss Cochrane scurried to avoid the stampede of children rushing for the front of the room.

Holly shuffled toward her bag and tried to look nonchalant, as if she hadn't the slightest interest in what rested in the bottom of the white sack. It felt light as air when she unfastened it from the chalk tray, and she forced herself not to look inside until she had gotten back to her desk.

Around her, the giggling popular girls struggled to keep their towering mounds of Valentines from floating to the floor. Holly's heart reluctantly filled with envy as she watched them. She wondered what it was like to have perfect hair and a bag stuffed full of Valentines. She looked down at her own white bag, its paltry contents mocking her.

One by one, she opened her cards and read the messages scrawled within. There was one from her teacher and a couple from two of the other quieter girls in the class. Holly peered into the bag and saw one more card resting on the bottom, like a pearl nestled on its oyster pillow.

The cocker spaniel on the baker's bag watched her trembling fingers unfold the pink paper and gasp in surprise.

Do you like me? Circle one:
Yes or No
Love, Brian F.

A blush redder than a heart-shaped box of chocolates crawled all the way up to her hairline as she looked across the room at Brian Foster. He looked back at her hopefully. Holly smiled, gave him a little wave and nodded ever so slightly.

Fifteen years later, Holly looked at the familiar writing on the crinkled pink paper and grinned. She wondered if Brian remembered writing that question so many years ago. She wondered if he thought about the note when they went to the homecoming dance in tenth grade, slow danced at the prom together their senior year, or drove home from college together for the holidays. Well, she would make sure he remembered this year.

This would be their first Valentine's Day together since she had moved back to their hometown from veterinary school last spring. Their first Valentine's Day as a serious couple. Brian's note from fifth grade would be the ideal gift.

Holly folded the pink paper back into its original shape, carefully placed it in a tiny box, and tied it with glossy pink ribbon. Perfect. The doorbell rang and Holly's stomach fluttered with anticipation.

"Brian! Happy Valentine's Day." Holly ushered him inside and tried to ignore the feeling of letdown when she saw his empty, flowerless hands.

I'm making too big of a deal out of this whole Valentine's Day thing. Holly chastised herself and wished she hadn't resurrected the fifth grade card. But it was too late. Brian was already tearing open the box.

For a moment, he just stared at the note and didn't say a word. Then, a lone tear slid down his cheek.

"Oh, Holly." He wrapped his arms around her and buried his face in her sweet-smelling hair.

"Do you remember that note?" Holly whispered in his ear.

"Of course, sweetheart! Did you think I would ever forget?"

Brian slowly released her, his eyes glittering. "Get ready for your gift now."

He disappeared outside and returned a moment later, struggling with an awkward white box sporting a red satin bow. The package seemed to have a life of its own. Holly lifted the lid and an adorable, doe-eyed, cocker spaniel puppy looked up at her from the box.

"Oh, Brian!"

When she lifted the puppy to cradle it in her arms, Holly noticed the pink scroll tied to its collar. She unrolled the spool and felt as though she were back in Miss Cochrane's classroom when she saw the familiar handwriting:

Will you marry me? Circle one:
Yes or No
Love, Brian F.

Holly threw her arms around Brian, and the puppy yipped and pranced in tiny circles at their feet. It was the perfect Valentine's Day.

Roll With It

JANET BANNISTER

WHILE THE COMPUTER BOOTS up, I roll my shoulders and stretch my neck, like a boxer in the corner of the ring, waiting for the bell. I watch the tiny hourglass hovering in the middle of the monitor's screen and plan my strategy for the next chapter.

Finally, the hourglass changes into an arrow, and I am able to open my document.

I scroll through three hundred and forty-seven pages before I find where I left my characters hanging. I'm just beginning to lose myself in my fiction world when a voice breaks my concentration.

"Hey."

My breath escapes in a huff. "What is it, Ashley?"

"Don't call me that. I told you, I'm going by my middle name."

What is it with this crazy name thing of hers? I swivel my computer chair around to face her. "Okay, firstly, if I wanted to call you by your middle name, I would have made it your first name. Secondly, Delta is a family name, your great-grandmother's maiden name. I am *not* going to call you Delta."

"Whatever. Ashley sounds like a soap opera chick."

My eyes catch a glimmer of something sparkling between her shirt and jeans, and my stomach churns. "Is that . . . a *belly earring*?"

She laughs. "Not belly *earring*. Belly ring."

"Why would you do that? You're not into that kind of thing. Why are you acting so . . . so . . . crazy?"

She rolls her eyes. "Obviously, I am into this kind of thing or I wouldn't have done it. You really don't know me very well."

I squeeze my eyes shut and rub my temples. I have no control over her anymore. "Did you need something?"

She shuffles from one foot to the other. "It's about California."

"What about it? You're not going."

Her voice is quiet, but firm. "Yes. I am."

"Oh c'mon, Ashley. You couldn't stand being that far away from your family."

She stares at me, immovable.

"Ash—"

"Delta"

"Fine. Delta, but your mother will fall apart. How is she supposed to deal with this?"

"That's your problem. Not mine. I'm going, and you can't stop me." She darts from the room.

Slowly, I turn back to the computer, my mind pondering the probable outcome if Ashley . . . no, Delta, goes to California. Her mother will sink into depression. Things definitely won't turn out the way I had planned.

But sometimes, you've just got to roll with it.

I highlight my last few paragraphs and hit "delete." Then I begin to type.

Delta's mother clung to her, refusing to let the embrace come to an end.

Finally, Delta pushed away. She avoided looking directly into her mother's eyes, which shot guilt-rays into her soul, as only a mother's eyes can. She headed for the airport's security checkpoint.

"I'll call you when I get there . . ."

Three hours later, I've added two thousand words to my story. I'm amazed at the new direction things have taken. Delta's mother really needed to face life without her, and the trip west is leading Delta to make some interesting revelations about herself.

Keys jiggle in the door, and in walks my Chelsea. "Hey. Get much written today?"

"Yeah, I didn't do too bad. I renamed Ashley. She's Delta now."

Chelsea grabs a glass and heads for the water dispenser. "Cool. Ashley sounds kind of like a chick in a soap opera."

My jaw drops. "Honey, you still don't like body piercing, right?"

"Ew, no. Gross." She grins at me. "Why, Dad? You thinkin' of getting your nipples done or something?"

I shake my head. "No, I don't think so."

My heart rate slows to normal as she sits beside me at the table and flips through the pile of mail she brought in with her.

"Hmm." She tears open an envelope. "Check it out. This is from that Bible school in California I told you about. I emailed and asked for information."

I let the possibility sink in. Strangely, it is peace, not fear, that fills my heart. I am not in control of my baby's life. Far from it. I'm not able to simply delete her dream of attending college three thousand miles away because I am not the author of her life.

But I know the Author, and He is in control.

I reach over to the computer and close my document. Then I lean in close to Chelsea. "So, tell me about this school."

The Girl Under the Bridge

Debbie Roome

❧

You have searched me, Lord, and you know me.
You know when I sit and when I rise;
you perceive my thoughts from afar.
Psalm 139:1-2

❧

WRITER'S BLOCK. FUNNY HOW it attacked at inopportune times. Pastor Thomas Berry gazed at the lines of fluid script written on the back of an old envelope. The topic had seemed so promising, so inspired, and yet the words had run out.

"Don't forget to put out the trash, dear." Eleanor padded past his study door.

Thomas sighed. Maybe a breath of fresh air was what he needed.

He swept the envelope from his desk top into the bin and went to empty the trash.

❧

It was a windy day out there.

A couple of miles from the dump, a young girl lay sprawled under a bridge. Tossed there like human refuse, eyes vacant, skin ravaged by drug and alcohol abuse. The vortex of addiction and prostitution had sucked life from her bones and drained her soul. Time no longer had any meaning for her. How long she'd lain in the rancid puddles she didn't know, but her will to live had gone.

"God," she whispered, "I'm sorry I've ended up in such a mess. I'd rather be dead than live like this anymore." Her right hand cradled a rusty blade she'd found lying under the bridge. "Forgive me, God."

The bridge shuddered slightly as a garbage truck approached, heavy with its load. A bag, ripped by a shard of glass, lay limp in its jaws, spilling papers, milk cartons, a handful of crusts, and a crushed deodorant can as the truck bounced along.

A sudden gust of wind lifted a crumpled envelope from the clutter, and like a crippled bird, it flew drunkenly upwards before fluttering slowly back to earth and dipping beneath the bridge.

～⋘⋙～

The blade was poised over her wrist, but before she could act, something dropped gently onto her chest. A dirty, stained envelope. The gracefully scripted words on the back jumped out at her.

> *You are God's handiwork, created by Him*
> *Formed by Him in your mother's womb*
> *He has not forgotten you*
> *He loves you with an everlasting love*
> *A love that will not let go*
> *God is a God of second chances—*
> *don't give up today*
> *Call to God and he will answer you*

They were streams of refreshment to the parched wilderness of her heart.

～⋘⋙～

Pastor Thomas Berry opened the door to find a young girl huddled against the door jamb. A sprite with tangled hair and filthy clothing.

With trembling hands, she pushed a muddy, crumpled envelope toward him. On one side was his name and address, and on the other, he recognized his own handwriting.

"Is it true?" she whispered. "Am I really God's handiwork? Will He really give me a second chance after the terrible things I've done?"

～⋘⋙～

> *I praise you because I am fearfully and wonderfully made;*
> *your works are wonderful,*
> *I know that full well.*
> Psalm 139:14

A Letter from Christ

Pat Guy

ASHLEY STRUGGLED TO CONTAIN the scream of anguish welling up from the depth of her soul, but she could not hold back the tears pouring down her cheeks. She had just miscarried—a crushing blow to her heart after years of effort. The doctor's words of try again seemed far away from the reality of her despair.

When my heart is grieved . . . you hold me by my right hand.[1]

The doctor marveled at the strength beyond this couple's unimaginable sorrow—a power beyond themselves.

He left them to their grief, wrapped in a love he could sense was present.

George gunned the accelerator. *No way is that car getting past me. Serves 'em right for tailgating.*

As the car pulled up beside him, George looked to the left, ready to gloat at the driver he had pinned in traffic. Instead, he was struck by the young girl's face of panic and tears. He saw a baby strapped in the back seat—too calm, too quiet, with blazing-red cheeks.

In your anger do not sin.[2]

The girl couldn't believe it. The man was slowing down to let her through. She instinctively turned to look at the driver and saw the expression on his face. She was so glad he wasn't angry. She just had to get to the hospital!

Twenty! That's what the sign says, lady! Twenty items—not fifty! Can't you read? Sheesh! Madison gripped the bar of the cart and clamped her mouth shut.

She seethed with the desire to say something to this elderly lady taking her time trying to fit what seemed like fifty items on the small space at the express lane. She struggled to keep her body language in check, too. One big, exasperated sigh would get the point across.

. . . help the weak, be patient with everyone . . .[3]

The elderly woman was aware of the controlled restraint of the young lady waiting next in line behind her. She appreciated it. It was her first time going to the store alone after such a long recovery. She wondered if her memory had been affected somehow; she didn't remember the counters being so small. Nevertheless, she smiled at the young lady and thanked her for her patience.

⁓⁓⁓

Thanksgiving—a time for feast and family.

As Mia flitted around the grocery store, she noticed a couple dutifully using a calculator, making sure every penny counted. She could tell they were facing hard times by their attempt to appear presentable in soiled, stained clothing . . . and by the empty look on the wife's face.

The young man smiled at Mia as she walked by with her cart half full. She flinched at the "buy one—get one free" bologna among the other few "staples" in the couple's cart. She heard the young man give a running total when the wife picked up another item. It went back on the shelf.

Therefore, as we have opportunity,
let us do good to all people . . .[4]

The young wife turned at the tap on her shoulder. She had almost finished putting their food on the counter. The lady with the smile gave her an envelope, along with a star ornament, mumbling something about Thanksgiving and Christmas.

She handed them to her husband and continued with the groceries, but when he showed her what the envelope contained, she was astonished.

Quickly she scanned the store, but the lady with the smile had disappeared somewhere among the aisles.

⁓⁓⁓

It has been said that you are the only Bible some people will ever read. Maybe the person who said that didn't realize they were paraphrasing from God's own Words:

You show that you are a letter from Christ,
the result of our ministry, written not with ink but with
the Spirit of the living God, not on tablets of stone
but on tablets of human hearts.[5]

A letter from Christ to the world. Yes, that's what we are . . . written in the blood of the Lamb.

~~~

[1] Psalms 73:21-23
[2] Ephesians 4:26
[3] 1 Thessalonians 5:14
[4] Galatians 6:10
[5] 2 Corinthians 3:3

PART SEVEN

Gone Fishin'

Them What Got Away

Kenn Allan

Welcome aboard! I yam Ol' Cap'n Biff,
An' th' *RUDDERLESS I* be th' name of me skiff—
Kindly step to the stern an' git moored to a pew
An' I'll tell ye 'bout fishin' fer men—like I do.

I've been sailin' these waters afore ye was born
From the Berth of Perdition to Gabriel's Horn—
I knows every trick of them fish in the sea
So thar's no better fisher to teach ye than me.

If it's Shallowtail Snapper yer crave to reel in,
Ye jus' cross-bait th' hook with a big glob of sin
An' then dangle it lively in front of th' nose—
They'll snap it right up! Down th' gullet it goes!
When th' hook finds its mark an' the sea billows red,
Ye kin use th' Good Book to whump hard on its head;
I've hear'd they quit fightin', roll over, an' float . . .

Tho' I've never yet gotten one into me boat.

An' here's a grand tip if ye happen to find
A Lost Mackerel school of th' holier kind—
Persuade 'em their method of swimmin' is wrong
'Cause th' fins they've been usin' are too blasted long.
When they splash up a fuss, ye jus' criticize louder
An' soon ye'll be swimmin' in Mackerel chowder!
Yer young'uns kin feast on th' portions ye'll waste . . .

Tho' as of today I've had nary a taste.

Beware th' Black Swordfish whot lurks in th' south—
He kin slice up an' parry each word from yer mouth;
Fer three nights an' a day we once shared glancing blows
Whilst I tried to grab hold of his well-informed nose.
If I had've knowed more 'bout th' wiles of that beast,
I might stayed thar a-scrappin' . . . instead, I released . . .
Thar's no tellin' whot evil he's spawned 'til this day . . .

Tho' I've spotted him since . . . he's been too far away.

But as a landlubber, ye might want to start
With a less feisty fish whot be fainter of heart—
Some Suffer-Faced Flounder should suit ye jus' fine
'Cause they hanker fer love an' bite hard on th' line;
Once ye heave 'em aboard they ain't much worth pursuin',
Unless coddlin' fish is a thing ye likes doin'—
With gentle persuadin' I've hear'd they rebound . . .

Tho' the ones I have ketched all git weepy an' drown'd.

Wahl, God bless me soul! Twilight shadows are stretchin'!
Thar's Groupers to gather an' Soles whot needs fetchin';
We've wasted th' mornin' with seafarin' talk—
Kin'ly untie me skiff once ye git on the dock,
Or iffen ye'd like, ye kin serve as my crew . . .

An' mebbe someday ye'll steer *RUDDERLESS II*.

On the Forty-First Day

JAN ACKERSON

*T*HE CURTAIN RISES ON Noah as he walks the decks of the ark. He stops by several animal enclosures and speaks in low tones. When he reaches the porcupines' pen, he stops, a puzzled look on his face.

NOAH: Shem! Come here, son. I want to show you something.
             Shem jogs to his father.

SHEM: What is it, Pop?

NOAH: Take a look at the porcupine. Does it look like he's missing several quills, there?

SHEM: Gee, Pop, I dunno. Ham's in charge of the porcupines. Get it? Ham? *Pork*-upines?
             Shem laughs heartily, pleased with his joke.

NOAH: (*sighing*) All right, all right. Where's Ham, then?

SHEM: Last time I saw him, he was on the top deck, getting some air. You know, Pop, now that the rain has stopped . . . it's getting pretty ripe in here. You can't blame him.

NOAH: (*another sigh*) Run along then, son. Go check on the cats, will you? They've been eyeing the mice recently.
             Shem exits and Noah climbs a wooden ladder to the upper deck, where he finds Ham sitting with his feet over the edge of the ark.
             Ham is holding a long stick, and there is a line dangling into the water. He has a bandage wrapped around his hand.

NOAH: What are you doing up here, Hammie?

HAM: You're gonna love this, Pop! I-I don't want to complain or anything, but I was getting kinda tired of those barley cakes Mom brought. 'What's for breakfast?' 'Barley cakes.' 'What's for lunch?' 'Barley cakes . . .'

NOAH: I get it, boy. Don't tell your mother, but I'm tired of them, too. (*They sit in pensive silence for a beat.*) So what's this, then?

HAM: I'm trying to catch a fish. (*With mounting enthusiasm*) I've got this
         stick, see, and I tied this line to it . . .
NOAH: (*very interested*) Where'd you get the line?
HAM: Yeah, about that. (*Sheepishly*) You might want to stay away from the
         back end of the mare for a while. Her tail might be a little bit sore.
         Anyway—I figured if I dangled this in the water, and a fish saw it,
         the fish might bite it, and I could pull him up. But . . .
NOAH: But what?
HAM: I needed something to hook the fish. So . . . (*he holds up his bandaged
         hand*) I visited the porcupines. I'm pretty sure quills grow back, Pop.
NOAH: Hammie, I'm amazed. What do you call this—this thing you're
         doing?
HAM: I've been thinking about that. How 'bout—fishing?
NOAH: No, no, that's not right. When I used to go hunting for deer, before
         the rain, I didn't call it 'deering.' I didn't call hunting for boar
         'boaring.'
HAM: Well, it was pretty boring.
         The two laugh at the pun.
         *There are several seconds of silence as they continue to gaze toward
         the water. Suddenly, something occurs to Noah.*
NOAH: How can you be sure the fish will grab that hook?
HAM: Bait, Pop.
NOAH: Not one of your mother's barley cakes . . .
HAM: Nah—fish don't like those, either. I used a worm.
NOAH: *What?* We've only got two!
HAM: Chill, Pop. We *had* two worms, forty days ago. There's a zillion of
         them now.
NOAH: Oh. Right.
         *Another minute of silence, then there is a flurry of activity as Ham
         struggles with the line. Eventually, he hauls up a fish, which flops on
         the deck at their feet.*
NOAH: So, how're we going to eat this thing?
HAM: Grilled? With some butter and onion?
NOAH: Son, I am not going to light a fire on this ark.
         They look at the fish again. It is draped in seaweed.
         I wonder . . . do you suppose your mother could cut it up real small
         and wrap it in some of that seaweed?

HAM: Raw fish? *Gross*, Pop.

NOAH: Well, let me know if you have a better idea, Mr. Fishing-With-Porcupine-Quills. Where's Japheth?

HAM: It's his turn for tiger litter detail.

NOAH: I'm going to go get him. I want you boys to do some more fishing. This just might catch on.

HAM: (*looking at the fish again*) It's kinda pretty, isn't it? Look at those colors, all in a row. We should call it a . . . I dunno. I've never seen anything with colors all lined up like that.

NOAH: (*eyes toward the sky*) It *is* pretty. Maybe the Lord God will show us what we should call it. It worked for Adam. Some kind of trout, maybe . . .

He exits, as Ham casts another line into the water.

Finding Neutrino

WILLIAM PRICE

~⚬✿⚬~

For since the creation of the world God's invisible qualities—
his eternal power and divine nature—have been clearly seen,
being understood from what has been made,
so that people are without excuse.

Romans 1:20

~⚬✿⚬~

HE HAD SPENT FOURTEEN years hunting for the secrets of the universe 2,500 meters under the Antarctic icecap. For most of his adult life, Wolfgang Armbruster had been fishing with the largest telescope on ice for the most elusive particle in the universe.

The scientist ran his rough fingers through his shaggy, graying hair. He gazed out his window at the blurred images of the Buenos Aires' Aeropuerto Internacional, as his jet roared down the runway. It was a long flight to Miami, and he was looking forward to a nice nap.

Sitting next to him was a six-inch-thick journal titled A.M.A.N.D.A. On the other side, the aisle seat was occupied by a woman in her mid-twenties.

"So, how long have you been working down in Antarctica?" The woman's voice was sharp and genuine.

The question startled Wolfgang. "Is it that obvious?"

She laughed. "There are a few clues. Your haggard beard and the red, weather-beaten face, with white, goggle-shaped circles around your eyes, are two indicators. Add to that a large notebook with an acronym on its cover, and I figure you've either been working on the icecap or hunting yeti in the mountains."

Wolfgang cracked a smile. "No yetis down there, but you're pretty perceptive, young lady. I spent most of the past fourteen years on Antarctica."

He cast a gaze at his inquisitor. "You a college student?"

"No, sir, I was down in Buenos Aires visiting my father. He's a missionary."

"That's interesting. What's your name?"

The woman giggled and smiled. "Amanda."

"You're kidding!"

"No, sir. That's my name. I've been dying to find out what that notebook is about. What does the acronym stand for?"

Wolfgang sighed. "The Antarctic Muon and Neutrino Detector Array."

"Okay, now what does it mean?"

The scientist shook his head and smiled. "You're going to make me talk this entire flight, aren't you?"

"Oh yes, sir. I hate to fly."

"Call me Wolfgang, then. Sir makes me feel old."

"It's a deal, sir . . . I mean, Wolfgang. That's a very scientific name."

"Probably because my father, Wolfgang, was a scientist, and his father's name was Wolfgang."

"Was he a scientist too?"

"No, he was a goat herder, but I was told he looked scientific."

They both laughed.

"So what exactly do you do?" Amanda asked.

"I fish."

"Is a neutrino a fish?"

"No, no. I've been fishing for secrets to the universe."

"In Antarctica?"

"Yes, deep under the ice, with a telescope."

"That's kind of backwards, but cool. You're searching for the secrets of Heaven inside the earth. And you're using an instrument that was designed to look outward, to examine inward. That could almost preach."

Wolfgang was puzzled.

"Forget it. It's just something my father says. So, what's a neutrino then?"

"It's a very energetic particle that is virtually undetectable. It doesn't have any mass or electric charge. One hundred trillion neutrinos pass through your body every second and you never know it."

"Why would you search for something you can't see or feel? Something that's for the most part invisible?"

"A scientist hates what he can't measure, but at the same time, is challenged to do so. Neutrinos are formed by some very powerful cosmic engine. Outer space is about ninety percent of things we cannot see. Neutrinos are part of that mystery. If we understand them, we might find hidden clues to the universe."

"Why search under the icecap?"

"Because it has little or no radiation to interfere with our detectors. You see, the earth blocks out the neutrinos with the highest energy, allowing the low energy particles to pass through. And then, about once a second, a neutrino collides with an atom and produces a subatomic particle that produces light. Our instruments can magnify the light one billion times."

"Do you have any pictures of those light explosions?"

Wolfgang quickly leafed through his notebook and showed Amanda a computer-enhanced image.

Amanda's mouth fell open. "That's amazing."

"Yes, it is."

"No, I mean, don't you see the face of Jesus?"

The scientist looked again, and his eyes widened with amazement. "My God."

"Exactly," Amanda exclaimed. "Your search of the invisible led you to its creator."

Wolfgang was silent for a moment and turned his gaze toward his travelling companion.

"I guess I'll be the one asking questions for the rest of this flight, Miss Missionary's Daughter."

"Imagine that." Amanda smiled and pulled a small Bible from her purse.

Flip-flops aren't for Fishing

TABIATHA TALLENT

A COUPLE OF YEARS AGO, a friend signed up for one of those internet dating services. She set up her page with pictures of her home and dogs, and wrote about her love for cooking, sewing, and shopping.

After the first couple of boring dates with overweight, middle-aged, depressed men, she decided to change her approach. She rented a small John boat and hired a photographer to take some pictures of her, down by her uncle's lake. The caption on her new web page read:

> Single, white, Christian female seeks Christian male
> who loves the great outdoors.

When she checked her page the next day, she had received fifty-two hits and a full box of mail. I sat with her as she looked at each response and the accompanying web pages. After a few weeks of emails and phone calls, she had a date set to go fishing with a man named Andrew.

Now, I have to tell you, my friend had *never* been fishing in her life. She had heard fish tales from her dad and my dad, and all of our friends' dads, but that was the extent of her fishing experience. She didn't know a fishing pole from a fishing lure, but she was determined to do whatever it took to avoid another boring "let's have dinner and talk about the weather" date.

She told Andrew that she had borrowed fishing gear for the picture, and he promised to bring everything she would need.

As we all know, first dates require a lot of planning for that perfect outfit. My friend faced a first date on a boat, in the middle of a murky lake, in high temperatures. She chose her favorite outfit: a pair of capris, a cute polka dotted top, and her favorite flip-flops.

Andrew picked her up at seven a.m. and they drove over to Sharpe Pointe. As the car ascended the curves of the mountain, she began to wonder how a lake could be that high. She was pretty sure that all the pictures she had seen of

Sharpe Pointe Lake had hills above the lake, so when Andrew stopped the car at the peak, she started to worry.

"Where's the lake?" she asked as he began to pull poles from the back of the truck.

"It's about a half-mile down the trail."

As you can imagine, my friend began to question her choice of clothing. She noticed that Andrew had worn old jeans and a t-shirt. He had told her to dress comfortably, but she didn't realize just how comfortably he meant. At this point, there was no escape, so she decided to suck it up and hike the half-mile down, flip-flops and all.

It didn't get any better down at the lake. The boat she had pictured with padded seats and cup-holders wasn't waiting near the bank. Instead, she had to sit on the grass, gravel, and dirt in her freshly ironed capris.

When she finally got settled, she was handed a hook and told that the best bait was fresh. The dirt between her toes didn't seem to matter much anymore. She had sunk to the level of playing with worms.

The date did get better. After realizing that she had pretty much set herself up for everything that happened, she decided to make the most of it. Andrew was a great guy and very understanding. He laughed when she told him how the picture from her web page came about, and even when she told him that she'd never touched a fishing pole.

They talked more than they fished, and decided they would try another date where she could wear her flip-flops more comfortably.

As I said in the beginning, that first date was almost two years ago. They spent many more afternoons getting to know each other on the sandy banks beside the lake. Andrew bought my friend a pair of shoes for fishing, she learned to appreciate fresh bait, and I got asked to be their maid of honor.

The wedding took place this afternoon on the grass in front of her uncle's lake. She and I wore sundresses and, of course, flip-flops.

Evangeline

Mo L.

"PLEASE, PLEASE, GREAT-GRANDPA." Pierre hopped from foot to foot beside the elderly man's chair. "Will you tell us again about the night you lost *Evangeline?*"

"Please?" added Pascal.

"Ah, yes." Great-Grandpa had a far-off look in his eyes. "She was the love of my life . . . until I met your Great-Gran of course."

"I'm not sure that's a good bedtime story," said Great-Gran.

"Nonsense," Great-Grandpa scoffed. "These kids should know their history. Now let's see . . .

"We had gone out for tuna, miles and miles out to sea. You couldn't just watch the weather on TV back then. No, you had to live it. We didn't have any of those electronic thingamabobs to tell you where you were, either. We navigated by the stars in the heavens. Which is why we were helpless when the blizzard hit, adrift at sea. Mountainous waves crashed over the deck, washing away anything that wasn't tied down. The whole lot of us almost perished.

"The storm lasted for days. The sails got wrecked. The mast was covered in thick, frozen sea splash. We were all sopping wet and so very cold. I've never been so scared in my entire life, not in ninety-two years . . . well, maybe on my wedding day." Great-Grandpa winked.

Great-Gran said, "Tsk!" Great-Grandpa liked to kid her, but she played a crucial role in his story.

"Where was I?" asked Great-Grandpa.

"You were adrift in the storm," said Pierre.

"With no hope," added Pascal.

"Ah, but we did have hope," said Great-Grandpa. "There's *always* hope, lads. There was nothing we could do to save ourselves, true. But we did more than just hang on for our lives. We prayed. And our prayers were answered. In the distance, between mountainous waves, we thought we saw a light. We aimed *Evangeline* for it, and prayed some more.

"By some miracle, we drifted closer to shore. Close enough for your Great-Gran to spot us out her kitchen window, high up on the cliffs overlooking the bay. She sent your Great-Uncle Philippe downtown to try to fetch us. Of course we were all quite young at the time.

"The storm had begun to break up, but it was still treacherous. Philippe rounded up some friends. They were fishermen, too. They knew what it must've been like for us, and for our families back home. It was crazy, really. No one goes out in a storm like that.

"It took all six of them to muscle their way through those waves to us. They had to constantly bail out that little boat, too. It was much too small for such heavy seas. They were soaked and half-frozen when they got to us."

"We'd beached *Evangeline* in a sandbar in the middle of the bay and dropped anchor, but we were stranded there, surrounded by the storm. Philippe and the fishermen helped us board the small boat.

"Because of Great-Gran's keen eye, and the bravery of Great-Uncle Philippe and the fishermen, not a soul was lost. But *Evangeline*'s anchor didn't hold. The tide was extra high because of the storm, and she was washed under and away. Even the sandbar washed away.

"*Evangeline* is still down there, way down deep in the bay, even today.

"You know, Philippe took us home, here, to Great-Gran, who had hot tea and soup waiting for us."

"And blankets and a warm bath," Great-Gran added "The mayor offered your Great-Grandpa a room in his manor, but he refused to leave his crew."

The old man smiled at his wife. "Great-Gran nursed me back to health. I had frostbite on the tip of my nose, but I'm lucky I didn't have much worse. Even now my nose gets awful cold and sore in the chill, but that's a small price to pay for all I gained."

"But you lost *Evangeline*," said Pascal.

"And isn't the captain supposed to go down with his ship?" asked Pierre.

Great-Grandpa tousled the red hair on Pierre's head. "If I'd gone down with the ship, I wouldn't have met Great-Gran, and you boys wouldn't be here.

"The Lord works in mysterious ways. You won't understand all the things that happen to you in this life. It can be hard sometimes, very hard. Life can be dangerous and terrifying and sad, but don't ever lose hope. He has plans for each of you, and in time, hopefully you will understand those plans.

"My plan, that day, was to catch some tuna." Great-Grandpa smiled. "God's plan was for Great-Gran to catch me!"

That J is a Hook

JAMES CLEM

$\mathcal{P}$AUL JOHNSON STEERED THE small motorboat around a half-submerged tree. This was a favorite fishing spot that his father had shown him long, long ago. He and Dad had come out to Lake Jeremiah on many occasions, and now Paul joyously passed the tradition on to the next generation. His mind flashed through treasured memories of a simpler time.

Paul's father had lived a Christian example for his two sons every day of his life, and had taught them the fundamentals of a solid faith. Paul lamented not seeing his brother Peter much anymore.

A random thought tumbling through his head caused him to smile. Dad had been pretty transparent in his hopes when he insisted his two sons be named for the two great apostles.

Paul's son, James, leaned over the front of the small boat, lifting his line up and around, trying desperately to keep it from getting tangled in the sunken branches. Paul guessed that tree must have a hundred hooks in it by now.

In the quiet of the early morning, Paul recalled his dad's favorite teaching, his passion in life that he shared with everyone. He would always begin with a simple line: "You just got to go fishing."

Whoever he happened to be talking to invariably smiled and looked him in the eyes—totally unaware of the sermonette that was right around the corner.

Dad would usually follow up with that corny, but true, old saying that "the worst day fishing is better than the best day at work." His companion would almost always nod or voice some type of agreement.

"You got to go fishing—it's in the Bible, you know." He would wink at them and they would be hooked. "It ain't no surprise that Jesus begins with a J. That J is a hook! He said 'I will make you fishers of men.' But the problem with Christians is that they just don't go fishing. They go to church and worship God—and that's a good thing. They might even sing in the choir, but that ain't fishing. I know lots of Christians who go to Bible studies and small group things to learn about fishing . . . and that's a good thing too, but again, that ain't fishing.

"People say, 'How come we don't see more people come to believe in Jesus?' And so I ask them, 'Where have you been fishing?' They usually have this strange look on their face, so I explain it like this. Jesus said, 'While you're out in the world . . . fish.' That's paraphrased of course.

"They have these new versions of the Bible today, with special notes and comments. We have Bibles for Promise Keepers, Women of Virtue, Kids For Christ . . . plus commentaries and study Bibles. I like to think of these as high-powered rods-and-reels.

"We also got the very best bait you could ask for—God's love shining in our own lives. That bait should be so strong that people are drawn to us; we don't even have to go looking for them. And the Holy Spirit will cause them to find us. We just have to be ready to fish. Where have you been fishing?"

Paul blinked and whispered, "I love you, Dad."

Breathing in deeply to drive back any tears, he called to his son, "Hey, James, let me tell you this story your Grandpa used to tell."

And He said unto them, "Follow Me,
and I will make you fishers of men."
Matthew 4:19 (KJ21)

Up from the Depths

ANN GROVER

THE APRIL SKY IS brilliant. Sun rays shimmer off the sea ice. I hold my harpoon at the ready, anticipating the emergence of a seal's glistening head from the air hole. I concentrate, trying not to think of my gnawing insides or my wife Qamaniq back in our snow house, with our baby tucked in the warm *amiut* against her back.

We need food. I haven't been able to catch any seal or fish for weeks, held in our snow house by blowing blizzards, unable to follow the caribou inland across the tundra, and unable to come to the sea, where ice has buckled into treacherous ridges, making it impossible to navigate the shoreline.

I think of the seal and my mouth floods, breaking my concentration. I must focus, keeping my eyes on the inky water, watching for telltale signs of an animal.

The sun hovers close to the horizon. Soon, it is too dark to see.

"Amaruq." Qamaniq whispers my name, and I pretend my belly is full for another night. Our baby plays on the caribou skin between us, his arms waving in the soft light from the *qulliq*.

In the morning, the men plan a fishing expedition. It is hoped we can get a whale. Nauja suggests we ask the *qallunaat* God for success.

I have no belief in the *qallunaat* God. The black-robed priest from the land to the south tells us a man, Jesus, died on a tree. How can this be? I have never seen a tree taller than a wolf, my namesake. Our trees are mostly gnarled twigs, just wicks for lamps. I must not ponder this foolishness for too long. It will muddle my mind and confuse my *ihuma*. I cannot allow that to happen. I may trip and land on my spear or fall in a crevasse.

Some of the men bow their head while Nauja says some words. I take note of the clouds and a few gulls overhead.

Finally, we set out, intoxicated by hunger. We pull the *umiak* into the laneway of open water and several of us take up oars.

The black-robed man also told us he is a fisher of men. I give my harpoon a doubtful glance. Did he intend to lance us with the harpoon? The fish spear? What kind of God do the *qallunaat* serve?

The heaved and twisted ice recedes, and we dodge floes as we head for open water. The man in the bow watches for blowing spray, a shining swell, any sign of whale, while the rest of us row.

"Amaruq, you are troubled." Nauja's voice comes between a pull on the oar.

"I am hungry."

"You are distressed from the prayer."

"I think nothing for the prayer."

"God is a mighty God."

"You are a fool, Nauja."

"*Immaga.*" Perhaps.

The *umiak* rises on the green-black swells, then is engulfed in the trough. Up and down, rising and falling. I could sleep. My eyes are very heavy.

"Whale!"

We are instantly alert. Our harpoons are drawn and, one by one, are flung into the glistening hide. The lines grow taut, and seal-skin floats bob into the icy sea. The *umiak* gives a jerk as the whale dives. I'm not prepared.

Icy saltwater closes over my head as my caribou parka pulls me under. Already my arms and legs feel leaden, and I sink deeper, deeper into the deadly, dark Arctic sea. I see through blurred green vision that Nauja is standing in the boat, his harpoon raised, aiming not at the whale, but at me. Perhaps it is a trick of the light, of the water.

He releases the harpoon.

I feel the impact.

There is no pain. So, then, this is what it is to die.

Then I am lifted over the side of the *umiak*. The harpoon is pulled from the thick hide of my caribou parka.

"I am a fisher of men, Amaruq."

I am silent.

The men pull the whale alongside the boat. Not a large whale, but it will feed us for a few weeks.

~ ✻ ~

Qamaniq mends my parka.

I still know nothing about big trees, but I know about being saved.

Ralphie's Angling Adventure

BETTY CASTLEBERRY

$\mathcal{I}$T IS VERY EMBARRASSING to appear in the emergency room with a fishing lure stuck in your hip. People have a hard time believing how it happened, but every word of it is true. I'm a pastor, so I shouldn't be less than truthful with you.

My wife Susan and I had decided to keep her nephew, Ralphie, for the weekend. Actually, she decided. She pleaded with me. "Please, Dan. How much trouble can a five-year-old be? Besides, you know my sister needs a break."

Ralphie showed up Friday night, carrying a little bag and a dump truck. Instead of watching my usual Friday night westerns, we watched a *Sponge Bob* video.

Susan entertained Ralphie the next morning, then asked if I would take him fishing with me. Saturday afternoons are my escape. I go to the lake to recharge my batteries and have some quiet time. I really didn't want to take Ralphie along, so I was prepared to be firm.

That lasted about two minutes.

I did warn Susan that I would have to stop by the church first to take care of some things for Sunday, and confirm a baptism as well. The church custodian was supposed to start filling the baptistery that morning, so I would have to check on that.

After lunch, tackle box in hand, Ralphie and I stopped by the bait shop and bought minnows. At that stage, I probably could have skipped the fishing altogether, as Ralphie was very excited about the minnows. Honor got the best of me, though, so I decided to take care of business at church and then take Ralphie to the lake.

When we got to the church, I set the minnows inside, explaining to Ralphie that the truck would get too hot and they would die. Then I checked the baptistery. It was almost full and had started heating. I needed to go to my office for a while, so I sat Ralphie down in the front pew with a roll of Life Savers®, and told him I would be back shortly.

My office was right next to the sanctuary, so I didn't think there would be a problem. Besides, if I left the door open and craned my neck around just so, I could see Ralphie.

I read a note from my secretary and returned a phone call. I had been in my office about fifteen minutes when I heard giggling coming from the sanctuary. I twisted around in my chair, but couldn't see Ralphie.

I walked out of my office and stood for a minute, staring at the baptistery. There was Ralphie, with his back to me. A million thoughts went through my head.

I hurried to him and saw exactly what he was doing. The minnows were in the water, and so was his Sponge Bob fishing pole. I watched as his face fell and he stopped giggling.

The minnows began bobbing to the surface, one by one, belly up. The water was much too warm for them. Ralphie threw a handful of Life Savers® into the water after them. For just a moment, I was angry, but when I saw the sad look on Ralphie's face, I couldn't stay mad.

I spent the next several minutes fishing dead minnows and Life Savers out of the baptistery. When I finished, I led Ralphie to a pew, and decided to have a talk with him. After listening to what the water was going to be used for, he innocently asked, "If it gives you new life, why did it kill the fish?"

Obviously I had missed the mark somewhere.

I explained that the water was only symbolic, and then, satisfied that I had made my point, I shifted in the pew. A stabbing pain shot into my hip. I jumped up and discovered a fishing lure embedded in my hip.

Ralphie again.

As hard as I tried, that lure would not come out. That's how Ralphie and I ended up in the emergency room on Saturday afternoon. When I told the nurse what happened, she could barely keep from laughing.

As soon as Ralphie left on Sunday, I went to bed. Susan felt guilty because she asked if there was anything she could do for me. I had her call my secretary and inform her I wasn't coming in Monday morning. Then I asked Susan to have her post a note on my office door:

"Gone Fishing . . . *ALONE*."

Caught

MELANIE KERR

This place that's so still
This sea that's so calm
Should be to my soul
A soft soothing balm

With fingers engaged in
An old welcomed task
"Where is the peace
And contentment?" I ask

I know I'm not waiting
Where He told me to stay
But on a boat fishing
In this place far away

There should be such joy
When I look on His face
But here I am hiding
Soiled by my disgrace

His words of forgiveness
Were not meant for me
If you knew my crimes
I'm sure you'd agree

I watched from a distance
The cruelty and hate
Reducing a man
To a pitiful state

This man was no stranger
But one I called "friend"
Someone I deserted
Denied at the end

"Have you caught any fish?"
A shout from the shore
The voice is familiar
I've heard it before

Without hesitation
And grabbing my coat
I hurl myself forward
And jump from the boat

At once I am swimming
Against a strong tide
Compelled by a passion
That churns deep inside

Does He still love me?
I hunger to know
Unless He commands me
I know I won't go

His hand reaches out
And He smiles at me
My guilt's wiped away
Unfettered—I'm free

"Oh yes, Lord, I love you
You know that it's true
I offer my life and
My heart up to you.

"Your lambs will be safe
Under my watchful care
For each of Your children
I'll always be there.

"Lead me, dear Shepherd
With you I will go
And tender devotion
To you I will show."

Sammy the Salmon

ALLISON EGLEY

"So what happened to you?" Sammy asked the halibut waiting beside him in the Saint Seaweed Hospital emergency room.

"Fishing accident. What about you?"

"Shark attack."

"*Whoa*! How did you get away?"

"It was close, let me tell you." Sammy's eyes widened. "I was swimming around, minding my own business, when I saw him. I kept swimming as fast as I could, but he kept gaining on me. Just as he was about to clamp down, I switched directions. He only nipped my fin. See?"

"Wow. Do you think you'll swim again?"

"Oh, sure. I've seen fish with worse injuries than mine swimming around just fine. Do you remember that fish in the news a few months ago? He nearly had his whole fin torn off."

"Oh yeah! I remember that. How's he doing now?"

"I heard they fixed his fin, and he's swimming around just like he used to. If they can fix him, I'm sure they can take care of me."

"Yeah . . . I'm sure you'll be just fine."

"So you said your injury is from a fishing accident?" Sammy looked skeptical. "I've heard of those, but I've never believed it. Sharks are what you have to worry about. Something as innocent as a worm can't hurt you."

"It can when it's attached to a hook. Look." The halibut opened his mouth wide. "See that hole in there? How else can you explain that?"

"Worms attached to a hook? That's stupid," Sammy scoffed. "You probably just bit your lip."

"Look . . . sorry," the halibut extended a fin, "I didn't catch your name. I'm Harvey."

"Sammy. Nice to meet you. Now, what were you saying?"

"I was going to ask why you think I would make up a story about a fishing accident if I just bit my lip?"

"Because you're too embarrassed to admit the truth."

"Suit yourself." Harvey flapped a fin at Sammy. "But I'm telling you, it was the worst experience of my life. I thought I'd caught a nice, juicy worm for lunch. Next thing I know, I'm being pulled up out of the water. I couldn't breathe. Then a monster grabbed me, looked me over, took the worm and hook out of my mouth, and tossed me back in the ocean. I could have died. I'm lucky I only have this hole in my mouth."

Sammy chuckled. "And that's where these fishing stories get preposterous. If you'd just told me you ate a worm and something sharp poked you in the mouth, I'd probably believe you. But no. All these stories involve fish getting pulled up out of the water, where they either disappear forever or claim to have had the same experience as you. Well, I don't believe it. There is nothing beyond this ocean. *Nothing.*"

Harvey narrowed his eyes. "Hey, I know what I saw and experienced. You don't have to believe me, but I wouldn't eat anything I didn't see swimming in the water first, okay? And if the same thing happens to you, and you feel yourself being pulled along, fight. Fight with all you have. I was one of the lucky ones. I survived."

"*Pah!* I'll do whatever I want."

Harvey shook his head. "Don't say I didn't warn you."

"Yeah, yeah. Whatever."

Days passed by, but Sammy kept what Harvey said at the hospital that day in the back of his head. He still wasn't sure he believed all these "fishing" stories, but he tried to be more cautious.

One day, however, the temptation was just too great.

"Hey, Goldie, look at that worm." It was the biggest worm Sammy had ever seen. "I'm going to bite it so hard it won't know what hit it."

"Ooh, I wouldn't do that if I were you." Goldie pulled back. "What about that halibut you met in the emergency room? Didn't he tell you not to eat anything you didn't see swimming around first?"

"Oh, come on. You don't believe that story, do you? Here I go."

"Sammy, don't!"

"Oh, this worm tastes so good. He's nice and big and—"

"Sammy, be careful!" Goldie's voice blubbed in panic. "I think I see something sparkling. It might be a hook, just like that halibut said."

"Goldie, you are so gullible. This is the best worm I've had in—ouch! *Mmph.*"

"Oh no! Sammy, find your inner Nemo! Can you still hear me? Fight, Sammy, fight! Swim down! Swim down! I don't want to lose you. No, Sammy! I can't reach—"

"Help!"

With a splash, Sammy broke through the surface of the water. "Can't breathe," he gasped. "Must . . . get . . . back . . . into water."

But it was too late. Harvey's monster grabbed Sammy, looked at him, and tossed him onto a pile of other victims.

"Harvey was . . . right," Sammy panted. "I should . . . have . . . listened . . ."

Sammy's last words were wasted, however. He could only hope everyone would believe Goldie. He didn't want to die in vain.

⁓❧⁓

> *The way of a fool is right in his own eyes,*
> *but a wise man is he who listens to counsel.*
> Proverbs 12:15 (NASB)

PART EIGHT

Let's Get Physical

Making a Difference

JAMES CLEM

*M*Y ADRENALINE SURGING, I pause before stepping into the batter's box. Our team is behind by three runs and down to our final two outs. Todd, our runner on first base, gives me a fist sign to slug it out. Glancing back, I see our best slugger, Steve, taking practice swings in the on-deck circle.

I scan the field to check the outfielders; they're playing deep—expecting me to try to smack one out. I smile inside as I find the gap between first and second. I want the homerun, but a sure base hit will give Steve a chance . . . and he's the tying run. A long fly ball that doesn't clear the fence is just an out.

I watch the first pitch, a called strike, to gauge the speed of the pitch. I'm ready for the second pitch when it comes. I swing early to push it to the right side. The first baseman dives for it, but he can't get it. Todd rounds second and coasts into third.

The fans are screaming enthusiastically as Steve swaggers confidently to the plate—a homerun will tie it up.

The pitcher turns around to scan his defenders, taking a deep breath before stepping back onto the mound. He winds and throws, and Steve hammers the pitch into right field. Todd trots home, and I readily move around second to third.

Looking over my shoulder, I see Steve turning it on—he's going to try to stretch it to a double.

The outfielder throws hard to second but Steve slides in under the tag.

Now Marcus is coming to the plate. He's pumped! Marcus is a power hitter; he'll be swinging hard. I hope he hits the ball and doesn't strike out.

I look to the on-deck circle and see Jim standing there—the worst hitter we have. My heart clutches, and I'm thinking, *Come on, Marcus; hit it out!*

Marcus swings at the first pitch. He's under it; all that adrenaline increased the speed of his swing. It's going deep to the outfield but it won't get out of here. I'm poised at third—as soon as the ball is caught, I can sprint home and Steve will come into third. Maybe Jim will somehow get a hit.

I score. Turning back to the field, I'm astounded to see Steve not stopping at third but coming full speed for home. Time slows down as the throw comes in. Steve launches himself head first. If he's safe, we're all tied . . . and if he's out, the game is over.

My mind races—I've known Steve a long time, he's fiery, stubborn, and headstrong. If they call him out, he's going to come up with fists flailing everywhere.

In slow motion, the umpire throws up one arm, indicating "Out." Surging hope implodes like a popped balloon. I quickly move forward to restrain Steve, but some *Twilight Zone* Steve gets up, saying to the catcher, "Nice tag—way to hold onto the ball."

I stare as he heads toward the dugout. I'm just close enough to hear him say to Jim, "Sorry, Bud, I should have held at third. You would have hit me in."

Jim didn't say anything, and I wasn't at all sure if he was disappointed or relieved.

I yell after Steve, "Hey, man! I was sure you would come up arguing that call. I've played with you for years. No one hates to lose more than you do. And you didn't say a word. This just isn't like you."

Steve looks at me for a long moment, showing a tinge of sadness that has nothing at all to do with the game. "No, Smitty, the old Steve would have done that, but not anymore—not since Jesus became the center of my life. I don't do that anymore. I'm a changed man. I mean, I still like to win, and I go all out on every play, but winning isn't the important thing, you know.

"We're a Christian team in a city league. We pray together as a team before and after every game. We don't pray to win, but that somehow people can see, by the way we play, that Jesus makes a difference. It doesn't work to preach at people, you have to show them a difference."

I wonder at that all the way home. I wonder if anyone can see Jesus making a difference in my life. I wonder . . . and I pray.

Gold Medal Gilbert

LORI OTHOUSE

~⟨⟨⟨❖⟩⟩⟩~

"*A*ND WE'RE BACK WITH our coverage of the 2024 International Non-Denominational All-Church Games. I'm Rebecca Stone, reporting live from the final day of competition where we've seen some tremendous displays of skill.

"I'm here with the five gold medalists from today's events. Let's meet them now."

The camera pulled back to reveal the winners, their gold medals gleaming in the late afternoon sun.

"Here we have the first place winner in the Running at the Mouth event, Fiona Flapgums! Congratulations, Fiona."

Fiona stepped forward and bowed dramatically, blowing kisses and waving.

"Next we have the winner in the Dodging Responsibility event—Dudley 'not my job' Deadbeat."

Nodding toward the camera, Dudley gave a quick wave.

Rebecca continued exuberantly, "And, of course, we have our champion in the Conclusion Jump—Fred Factless. Way to go, Fred!"

Fred grinned, holding up his medal and mouthing "Thank you" to the camera.

"Our next event is somewhat new, but gaining popularity fast. First place in Throwing Under the Bus is Betty Backstabner."

Clasping her hands in the air, Betty beamed victoriously.

"Our final competitor is from an event that, after this year, will no longer be featured at the All-Church Games. Receiving the gold in Fighting the Good Fight of Faith is Gilbert Godly."

Gilbert smiled politely at the camera.

"So, Gilbert," Rebecca began, "since we won't be seeing your event again, do you have any parting words for us?"

Looking past the camera into the crowd, Gilbert answered, "I'm very, very disappointed that Fighting the Good Fight of Faith is being eliminated. I feel it's probably the most important event, and without it, I don't know what will happen within the church."

There was a huffy snort from Fiona, followed by the buzz of whispering.

"Well," Rebecca smiled, continuing, "many people say with the rapid advancement of technology and healthcare in recent years, the event is outdated and unnecessary. That as a culture we've grown beyond the need for 'old-fashioned' faith. How would you respond to that?"

"Faith is absolutely necessary if we are to survive as Christians. The Bible says that without faith it is impossible to please God. His Word is never outdated because God is never outdated. No amount of technology can replace faith in the God of the universe."

"Gee, Gilbert, maybe you should have entered the Preaching to the Choir event!" Rebecca giggled, amused with herself, but seeing Gilbert's sad stare, she quickly regained her composure.

"Uh . . . obviously you are a man of some conviction. So what will you be doing now?"

"Oh, I'll keep fighting . . . fighting for a greater prize. I just hope I won't be the only one."

"Sure! Sounds great!" Rebecca gave a saccharin smile. "Keep on keeping on. Maybe you can return in one of the other events."

Gilbert looked over toward the other medalists. "I don't think so," he answered quietly.

"Well, we wish you—*all of you*—the best! And a big congratulations to all our competitors; you're all winners.

"This is Rebecca Stone with Channel 5 News. Good night."

Voices of the Game

AMY MICHELLE WILEY

WESTBROOK, MAINE

The radio boomed through the open family room windows, filling the backyard with sound. Jimmy yelled even louder, holding an imaginary microphone to his mouth as he echoed the sports-caster.

> *"This is it, folks! This is the game we've been waiting for.*
> *The Yankees face the Red Sox in just one minute!"*

"Positions!" Dad waved his hands at his spread-out family. "Adam, you're up to pitch first."

> *"Donnelly up to bat . . . Farnsworth pitches. Donnelly*
> *swings. Solid double! It's off to a great start, folks!"*

AUSTIN, TEXAS

Lissa slouched in the back of the church, wondering what had possessed her to come. Whoever heard of watching a baseball game in a church anyway?

The sudden cheer of the crowd startled her as the ball on the screen soared high, a tiny white dot against the sky. Just a speck, easily unseen, easily unnoticed.

> *"He's rounding first base and headed for second. The*
> *outfielder is scrambling for the ball . . . he's got it!"*

"Hello, are you new here?"

Lissa jerked her eyes away from the screen. "Oh, yeah, I guess." Someone had noticed her?

"I'm June, and I'm glad you came."

> *"Donnelly slides . . . he's safe! Just in the nick of time!"*

BEAVERTON, OREGON

Jenna only knew a couple of the teens filling the room. She perched on the folding chair, avoiding eyes, pretending to watch the game. She fought the bile that rose in her throat, choking on the sickly-sweet smoke that clogged the air.

Maybe Kyle's parents would come home early. Her eyes found the front door, wanting it to open. Willing it to open.

"The bases are loaded! Mussina pitches."

A form stepped in front of the TV. Jenna looked up. Right into Kyle's blue eyes. Her heart flip-flopped. He held out a packet of white powder. She found herself reaching for it mechanically, ignoring the trembling of her hand.

She didn't bother licking her finger first—it was wet with sweat. The powder clung to her, thick as the guilt that weighed her soul.

"Pineiro swings. Foul ball!"

MANHATTAN, NEW YORK

A single tear dripped down Melanie's cheek, as if her heart had finally cracked and allowed a hint of emotion to seep through. For months now she had told herself everything was fine. She could handle it.

Melanie glanced at Jake, hunched toward the TV screen. Would he notice her if she shouted as loudly as the sports announcer?

"The crowd has gone wild! The Yankees are ahead by two runs! Watch carefully, America, this next pitch could decide the game."

Her sob was audible this time. She fell forward, her shoulders shaking with inner pain. Where was the joy of the American dream? Why was it so empty? What had she done wrong?

"Drew is having trouble today. We'll see if he can connect with the ball this time. Here it comes . . . it's a curve."

Jake didn't look up when she left the room. Didn't question her as she emptied her drawers, or even when she dragged the suitcase down the stairs.

She paused at the front door, wishing he would come. Straining to hear her name. Only one sound reached her ear.

"Three strikes. He's out!"

SAN DIEGO, CALIFORNIA

Daddy's voice was getting louder. It seeped through Ben's bedroom door, angry and snarling. Ben turned up the radio.

"The Red Sox still have a chance. Timlin's up to bat. Can he pull through for his team?"

The fist hit the wall first, setting Ben's models rattling and his heart pounding. He stood. Took a step toward the door.

"It's the ninth inning. Time is running out for Boston."

The fist was quieter this time. Sickening. His mother's muffled cry twisted his stomach. Tomorrow she would hide the bruise and say it was her fault, that she shouldn't have provoked him.

It came again. Ben froze. He could only stand and listen. Listen and wish it would stop. Wish it wasn't so.

Finally it did stop. But that was worse. Silence. What if Daddy had really hurt her bad this time? What if she was dead? Ben should have done something. He could've stopped it. Could've at least tried.

"Rivera pitches wild. Timlin holds. Ball three!"

He heard movement in the kitchen. Relief weakened his legs. She was okay. She'd made it through.

"The Yankees take the victory! That was a close game."

PENSACOLA, FLORIDA

MaryAnn's knees cracked as her feet tapped the floor, nudging the rocker into a soothing movement. "God bless America." Her voice mingled with the radio's eager appraisal of the game.

A gnarled finger wrapped a loop of yarn around her crochet hook and pulled it through. "Weave together Sammy's broken body, Lord." Another tug of the yarn. "As he wraps this blanket around his shoulders, let it remind him of your love. As he heals from the accident, let him use the time to draw closer to you."

"Next week the Yankees will take on an even tougher team.
Tune back in to see if they are up for the challenge!"

MaryAnn's hands stilled for a moment. Sammy had listened tonight, too; she was sure. He loved baseball. So many others, too. Others who needed prayer.

She clicked off the radio. Her attention returned to the blanket, her wrists twisting with more strength, her prayers rising with each loop. There was much work to be done—no time to waste.

I Saw Him

LYDIA PATE

I saw Him . . .
in the faces of the children for whom we climbed,
countless, nameless young souls
too sick, too vulnerable, too lonely,
too robbed of childhood joys and innocence,
and for them Jesus died.

I saw Him . . .
in the rainforest,
flush with downpours,
a shroud of lush, green foliage,
enveloping sounds of insects, birds, monkeys and falling rain—
send your heavenly showers, Lord, down on me.

I saw Him . . .
in the approaching dusk,
waves of fog encircling
and girding the mountain with silence,
blotting out the closing rays of sun,
but not His presence compassing me about.

I saw Him . . .
as I climbed,
through varied landscapes,
changing climes,
flaming flowers, soaring senecios, lofty lobelias,
all nature a portrait of His signature divine.

I saw Him . . .
in the rainbow at day's end,
foretelling His promise to not forsake me,
an arduous climb endured,
a test of character for sure—
He was my Guide and hovered o'er me as blissfully I slept.

I saw Him . . .
in the saddle,
barren lunar landscape,
inhospitable to life,
wanton winds raking from peak to peak.
Holy Spirit, come and blow upon my soul.

I saw Him . . .
in the midnight hour,
when at strength's end,
and yet a harder climb ahead,
my diminishing reserves I tallied and knew I needed more,
yet in my weakness was His strength made perfect.

I saw Him . . .
in the blush of sunrise
at eighteen thousand feet,
the sky His canvas,
His strokes of peach and coral awakening a faultless blue,
and then, a gilded copper sun heralding the morning.

I saw Him . . .
in the final thrust,
an indescribable moment in time
at nineteen thousand feet,
white-capped peak of gleaming snow and ice, ethereal beauty—
His creation sang His praises and shouted His glory.

I saw Him . . .
at the summit,
each oxygen-depleted breath consuming my strength and will,
my frailties driving me closer to His breast;
a greater path He had already walked—
He climbed a mount called Calvary!

～✧～

Reflections on climbing Mt. Kilimanjaro,
Tanzania, East Africa

A Day at the Gym

T.F. CHEZUM

"**N**OW WHAT?" JACK BLURTED, disgust echoing in his voice. He slid a yellow flier from under the windshield wiper: HOW MANY?

A quizzical expression crossed his face. "Stupid junk."

He crumpled the paper and tossed it to the back of the carport.

"The dumpster is at the other end of the complex." Mrs. Johnson gestured, reeling in her yapping Pomeranian.

Jack gave a sarcastic wave. "Whatever." He climbed into his Escalade, dropping his gym bag on the seat beside him.

Her scowl reflected in his rearview mirror.

"*How many?*" the radio blared as the engine fired up.

"Geeze!" Jack flinched at the unexpected greeting, cranking the volume down. He rested his Ray-Bans on his nose and drove off.

Jack pulled into the fitness center parking lot.

The driver of an orange Volkswagen put the top down on his car before pulling out of the stall; a little red Corolla waited behind. Jack whipped his SUV into the vacant parking space, missing by inches the convertible that had backed out.

"Hey! We were waiting for that spot." Joyce leaned out the window of her compact car.

Jack shrugged. "You snooze, you lose."

Stepping from the driver's seat, his foot slid on a torn newspaper; he glanced at the headline: PEOPLE.

He kicked it away from his car.

"You're such a jerk," the woman yelled, revving her engine as she drove off.

The treadmill droned.

"Are you almost done?" Kathy smiled, resting against an elliptical machine.

"I still got a couple of miles." Jack patted his brow. "Then a cool down."

"All the machines are taken." Her smile faded into a glare. "You're not supposed to take this long when people are waiting."

"Sorry, can't interrupt my training." He took a swig from his water.

"Forget it." She swung her arms in frustration.

Jack sauntered toward the pool, his towel draped around his neck. He paused for a moment, admiring his physique in the mirror.

"How many people?" a nearby walkie-talkie crackled, and Jack jumped at the sudden noise. Frank snatched the radio from the counter and stepped out of earshot.

Jack smoothed his hair and proceeded to the door.

"The pool's not available." Frank waved his arm, trying to get Jack's attention.

"What do you mean? I paid for my membership. I get my pool access."

"Sorry, senior water aerobics, and there's a lot of them today."

"Great!" Jack whipped the towel off his shoulders. "My workout gets ruined by a bunch of hapless geezers."

Frank stared in disbelief as Jack stomped off.

Tabitha stood up from the weight bench, stretching her arms over her head. The slogan on her shirt stretched into view: INFLUENCE.

Jack jumped to the barbell, adding weights to both ends.

"Hey, I was using that."

Jack sat on the bench. "You walked away."

"I was stretching between sets," Tabitha huffed. "I wasn't done."

"Oh, well. I won't take too long." He reached behind him and grabbed a towel. "I think you forgot this."

She snatched the towel from his grasp and stormed off.

Ron and Belinda stood, engrossed by the television. The video echoed through the snack bar. *"People will be influenced by . . ."*

Jack leaned across the counter, snapping his fingers. "Can I get some service?" he hollered.

"Sorry." Ron paused the tape. "She's pretty new. Just showing her a training video."

"Well that's very dutiful of you." Jack's words radiated disgust. "But I need a Triple Berry Blast, pronto." He gestured toward the preparation area. "And I want it done right, so don't let her touch it."

Jack snatched the smoothie from the counter and slipped his shades on as he walked out the door. A neon sign flickered to life: ACTIONS.

A honking horn didn't faze him as he stepped from the curb. He extended his flat palm toward the driver.

"Watch where you're going," Bill barked.

Jack continued to slurp his smoothie while strolling through the lot.

A green paper fluttered on the windshield of his Escalade.

"Not again." He ripped the leaflet from under the wiper and gave it a casual glance as he tossed it to the ground: YOUR ACTIONS.

⁓⟡⁓

HOW MANY PEOPLE WILL BE INFLUENCED
BY YOUR ACTIONS?

The Race in His Strength

Elizabeth Baize

I wandered in the misty night
Surrounded, but alone.
Despair was clutching at my heart;
My hope of life had flown.

I crumpled down upon my face;
My heart in earnest cried,
"Oh God above, if You exist,
Come now and be my Guide!"

With wonder flowing through my soul
I saw the darkness part.
A ray of light burst through the night
To shine into my heart.

A prayer of thanks I offered up,
"Oh Lord, my eyes can see!
The darkness has been sliced away;
I know You've set me free."

A voice then fell upon my ear,
"My child, rise, run your race.
But do not fear for I am near
To fill You with my grace."

Before me stretched a golden path
So narrow and so straight.
"My child, no matter what you see
You must not deviate."

"Yes, Lord!" I flew at lightning speed,
With joy ran down the trail.
But soon I sank down to my knees—
My weakness did prevail.

"Oh Father, I have failed again;
No strength in me remains."
"Yes child, your strength will fade away,
But mine always sustains."

"Then Lord, replace my feeble strength
With Your own mighty power,
That I may run and not grow faint
Again within the hour."

"Run then, my child. My strength is yours;
Endurance is the key.
And run with patience, faith, and hope
Until you're home with Me.

He gently raised me to my feet;
My race began anew,
Rejoicing in His strength alone
As down the path I flew.

But suddenly before me stood
A great and lofty wall.
I faltered with a mounting fear
That I would surely fall.

Perhaps there was another way
Around instead of over.
But then again I heard the voice,
"My child, don't be a rover."

"The path is straight. Just take the leap
And trust that you will fly
On wings that soar above, beyond
This wall that seems so high."

I leaped and hurtled through the air;
The wall beneath me lay.
"Oh Lord, increase my faith," I prayed,
"You've proved Yourself today."

Then onward in my race I pressed;
The way seemed smooth and plain
'Til up ahead a jagged cliff
Reared up with proud disdain.

I found myself right at the base;
The stones seemed smooth as glass.
"I'll never reach the top!" I cried.
"There must be some bypass."

"Now child, your path runs up this cliff.
I'll give you feet that cling
Like those of deer or mountain goats;
From rock to rock you'll spring."

"I'll trust You Lord." I set my foot
Upon the rocks to find
I climbed them with the skill and ease
God's grace for me combined.

In triumph I did reach the peak;
More mountains lay ahead.
But faithful was my loving Lord
As on and on He led.

But finally a mountain rose
More lofty than the rest.
And this one stood upon my path;
I knew it was a test.

This mountain was not made to climb;
Instead God had a plan
To show His strength was just as strong
As when my race began.

"Oh God above, if I have faith
The size of a small seed,
I know this mountain will remove
So that I may proceed."

The mountain shook from base to crest.
In awe I watched it slide
Into the very ocean depths;
My Lord was glorified.

Before me where the mount had stood
My path shone in the sun.
"May God above be praised today
For matchless deeds He's done!"

And up ahead I saw my Lord;
"He's waiting there for me!"
In humble adoration I
Did bow upon my knee.

"Well done, my child. You've won your race."
His hands were on my brow.
"The victor's crown is yours today;
With love I give it now."

I raised my hands and touched the gold
That stood for Race Complete.
Then took the crown won with His strength
And placed it at His feet.

Transition

Beth Muehlhausen

THESE GOGGLES ARE THE greatest! I can see the outline of the boat just fifteen feet away, even with foggy lenses. And there's the black inner tube skimming along behind, tied to that short length of rope. Not that I will need it. All those weeks of training have paid off. I'm going to succeed at this long-distance swim—the whole three miles from one end of the lake to the other.

Air moves in . . . out . . . in . . . out . . . as my face turns to inhale quickly near my left shoulder, and then toward the inky depths of the lake to exhale.

In . . . out . . . in . . . out . . . my breathing perfectly matches my crawl strokes. I must remember to completely expel each breath into the water every time in order to benefit from the oxygen in the next one.

Scissor kick, then flutter . . . reach, pull . . . my appendages work in harmony to propel me forward with synchronized ease.

My mother, clad in a sleeveless blue sundress and wide-brimmed straw hat, patiently monitors the ten horsepower motor on the back of the wooden fishing boat so it idles at a speed to match my pace.

My sister, eleven years my junior and a cheerleader type, periodically calls out encouragement from the bow: "Keep going! You can do it!"

Intuitively, I sense my heart beating in my chest with a steady, comforting rhythm. This is no more stressful than walking; surely I will go the distance.

In . . . out . . . in . . . out. For a moment, I wonder about being a foreigner. Is this what it feels like to be a fish—or perhaps a waterfowl that swims effortlessly and then flies through the air without encumbrance or resistance? Or is this the kind of tranquil union with one's surroundings that is felt at death, when the afterlife comes to encompass the spirit?

The noisy boat motor, which is almost fifteen years old, faithfully chugs along—and yet I can hardly hear it because of my earplugs. Every once in a while I glimpse sunlight reflecting like brazen diamonds on the choppy surface of the water. Ah, I am cutting through diamonds! Scooping them with my hands—flinging them through the water with each kick. They lie behind me, floating on the surface—or is that a trail of bubbles? My breath—has it been converted into sparkling dots?

I wonder how long it will take to complete this marathon at my current pace.

Pent-up pain and frustration expelled with each breath, each stroke, and each kick. Chronic issues evaporate: my less-than-feminine appearance, social inadequacy, poor organizational skills, fear of leaving home for college. None of that matters here.

Oddly, I feel myself relax in some deep, inner spot. This is like being in another dimension. I can be completely honest with myself and open to the experience.

In . . . out . . . in . . . out . . . in . . . out.

My muscles work; away go the anger and fear. My lungs breathe; in comes energy and confidence.

I'm free! I skim through the water . . . FREE!

Maybe my mother and sister are talking over there in the boat. I wonder what they think. Are they proud of me; do they believe I can do this?

It doesn't matter. I know I can. I can and I will. I *am* doing this!

In . . . out . . . what's that? My own heart is speaking? What?

You are so much more than you know; more than a young woman who struggles to measure up to expectations. Today you are learning how situations cannot trap you, because you are more than your circumstances. Today you will discover the truth. Today you will find yourself.

Oh! My heart . . . my soul! I can't afford to cry now—no. Keep steady.

In . . . out . . . in . . . out . . . in . . . out.

Trust myself; trust my heart; trust my breath. Keep going . . .

~⚬✾⚬~

I can envision all the details of that marathon swim, even though it happened almost fifty years ago. I blossomed after that day—emotionally as well as physically. I sense I am there again, right now . . . fit, trim, starting over, even as I lay in intensive care, connected to a respirator, ready to release my breath . . .

. . . and go Home.

Mulligan's Island

WILLIAM PRICE

MARGIE LINKWIDOW'S RIGHT ARM was in a cast. She held a cup of tea with her usable hand while she spoke with her mother at the kitchen table.

"We had to avoid two snakes. Not one, Mom, but two."

"What kind, dear?"

"I don't know. The ugly, I-want-to-bite-you kind."

"Is that when you broke your arm?"

"No, that came later. First, Frank had to climb a tree, fall in a pond, and dump our golf cart over on a steep hill."

"Did you break it then?"

"No, that's when I skinned my knee and broke a fingernail."

"I'm so sorry, dear."

Margie scooted her chair back from the table. "Do you see this bruise on my leg? Frank hit me with a golf ball. I was standing thirty feet directly to his right. It defied all laws of physics. We also got chased by a dog while we looked for another golf ball in somebody's backyard. And do you see this knot on my head? He hit me with a golf club."

"What?"

"Well, I thought standing in front of him was too dangerous, so I stood behind him and, *WHAM*, a seven iron right in the noggin when the club slipped out of his hands."

"Margie, dear, what about your arm?"

"I fell into a deep sand trap."

"What . . . why . . . how?"

"I thought standing on the far side of the green was the safest place while Frank was putting. But when he made it, I got excited, jumped up, and fell backwards into the sand."

"Margie, how did he get you to go golfing with him in the first place? Didn't I warn you? Golf is not included in the wedding vows. It's beyond worse; more deadly than any sickness. It's akin to death."

A smile crept across Margie's lips. "I'm sorry, Mom, but it was my fault."

"What do you mean?"

"We were watching golf on TV, and I told Frank it wasn't a sport. He told me there was a difference between professional golf and real golfing and invited me to go. So I did."

Her mother reached across the kitchen table and grabbed her daughter's hand. "It's okay now, dear. You survived. Just promise me you'll never go again."

"I won't, Mom. It's too dangerous."

"Margie, listen to me, and look at me when I say this. The danger of tagging along with your husband golfing isn't just physical. You might—and I hardly dare even speak the words—want to play yourself."

"And that would be a bad thing? Not that I would ever want to, but I know I could play as badly as he does."

"Stop! Stop that train of thought right now. Listen to me. Both of you playing would be the end of your marriage. You need for him to be gone golfing. And he needs to be able to come back home and tell you how low he shot. Men have a unique scoring system in golf. For some reason, all those shots they chase after in the woods and across airport runways, and fish out of ponds, don't count. They created a word called 'mulligan.' They're allowed to hit another ball and get a second chance, like the last shot never happened.

"Trust me. Take up bungee jumping, sky diving, anything but golf. Don't get sucked into their bizarre world."

"Did you ever golf with Dad?"

"I don't like talking about it, dear. It's too painful. But do you remember that summer you and I lived with Grandma and Grandpa?"

"Yes, was it because of golf? I thought Dad had to work and couldn't go on vacation with us."

"No, it was golf. I had begun playing and actually scored better than him. His friends started wanting me in their foursomes in tournaments. It was awful."

"What happened?"

"We separated."

"How did you get back together?"

"Church."

"Church?"

"Yes, dear, it was your dad's idea. Of course, if I had known there was a Christian Men's Golf League involved, I never would have fallen for it. But it worked out. It was the best thing that ever happened to our marriage and family."

"So, we didn't always go to church?"

"No, it all started with golf. In fact the married couples' home group we're hosting now is a result."

"Isn't that the group you want Frank and me to join? What's it called again?"

"Mulligan's Island."

Batter Up!

Marilee Williams Alvey

James sat on his bunk, hugging his knees and rocking.

"Better find a way to get yourself out of this cell, you worthless piece of garbage," his cellmate hissed, "'cause if you don't, you're gonna be missin' pieces. You won't even know who's comin' for ya 'til it's done."

K-Dawg's eyes were as cold as a marble slab. His massive biceps held the promise of pain.

"I don't want any trouble. I've got nothing against you. I'm trying to get in the college prep program." James winced. Not the right thing to say, but he wasn't skilled in talking to felons. Though he was one himself, now.

Meth had come courting James. The crystal ladder was thrown before him, promising no more shyness or awkwardness. In the beginning, he was confident, self-assured, and empowered. Then, too soon, the crystal ladder became a sticky spider web that engulfed him. He was lured in, and then strung out to die.

"College prep, huh? Better study mortuary, 'cause you're lookin' at the grave, maggot."

He played his internal tape once again. Sneaking, snatching, lying . . . just another meth addict with no borders. James proved it when he decided to hit a credit union for cash. Using pepper spray in the attack, he thought it wouldn't qualify as assault with a deadly weapon, but he was wrong to the tune of thirteen years.

At twenty-six, James found it impossible to imagine being thirty-nine.

He lay down in bed, and in desperation, began to pray. "God, I've made such a mess of my life. I don't know what to do. I'm scared. I'm so scared. Please don't forget me here."

He pretended to be asleep in an attempt to diffuse K-Dawg's anger. Eventually, James's breathing slowed and his eyelids got heavy. Sleep arrived, giving him a momentary reprieve from his cell.

He found himself sitting, once again, on a bench in his high school dugout. The air felt as hot as car exhaust. Sweat trickled down the front of his uniform, forming mud of the earth that clung to him. His catcher's mask and chest protector kicked up dust as he flung them to the ground.

Standing up, he grabbed three bats and began to swing them as he watched the pitcher. After several more practice swings, he selected his bat of choice and approached the batter's box.

Laying off the first pitch to see what the pitcher had, he heard the grunt of the umpire.

"Stee-rike one!"

James stepped out of the box and took several swings to stay loose. Stepping back in, he felt the adrenaline kick in. He swung as hard as he could. Whoosh!

"Stee-rike two!"

Stepping out again, James swung several more times, trying to remain loose and calm. Sweat dripped down into his ear canals. The crowd was yelling, but it sounded as if they were screaming underwater.

Stepping back into the batter's box, he steadied himself. Somewhere in the distance, his ears picked up desperate cries of, "It just takes one, James!" and "Keep your eye on it!"

The pitcher released the ball. It was a rocket headed straight for the strike zone.

James swung once again as the ball dipped suddenly.

"Stee-rike three! You're out!"

Shame made its bed in the pit of his stomach while self-condemnation made a nest in his heart.

James woke up breathing heavily, with the sweat-soaked sheet twisted around him. With relief, he realized it was five in the morning. K-Dawg would already be on duty in the dining hall.

He hung his arm over the edge of his bunk, feeling for the Bible underneath his bed. Looking up "discouraged" in the back, he found:

> *"The Lord himself goes before you and will be with you;*
> *he will never leave you nor forsake you.*
> *Do not be afraid; do not be discouraged."* [1]

"God, I'm stuck. There's no hope left in me. It's too late. I'm completely out of control of my life and I'm scared to death."

At that moment two guards appeared. One began to unlock his cell door. "Got some good news for you."

"Yeah?"

"Gather up your stuff. You're being transferred to the college prep wing."

"Now?"

"No, next month. Now, get goin'!"

Gathering up his belongings, James stepped into the batter's box once again. Walking out of the cell, and only for his Savior, he pointed toward an imaginary fence.

~✦~

[1] Deuteronomy 31:8

Battle on Ice

DOLORES STOHLER

*L*AURA'S HEART SWELLED WITH pride as she watched her teenage daughter whirl about the ice, practicing her leaps and spins. Already a champion, Dulcie was sure to be chosen for the Olympic team.

The rink was bare except for one other skater, Irina Tchakova, a tall girl who skated with less confidence, falling as she tried to pick up speed.

Laura watched as Dulcie skated over and bent to help Irina to her feet, but the other teen wrenched herself away.

"Don't you touch me," she screamed. "I hate you. How dare you be better than me?" To punctuate her angry words, she grabbed Dulcie by the hair, pulling her down on the ice beside her. With flailing fists, Irina knocked Dulcie about the head, making her scream.

"Get off my daughter!" Laura was horrified and hurled herself onto the ice. Slipping and sliding, she made her way over to the struggling pair.

Dulcie was fighting back, trying to hold Irina's hands to keep her from clawing her face. The blades on Irina's skates came dangerously close to kicking Dulcie's legs.

Reaching the fighting pair, Laura tugged Irina off her daughter while Dulcie struggled to her feet.

"What are you doing to my daughter?" It was Irina's mother. "Leave her alone." She turned to the grim-faced trainer beside her. "That girl tried to harm my daughter. I saw the whole thing. She tripped her up when she skated by."

Laura's mouth flew open in surprise. "She did no such thing. You weren't even around. Did you see Irina attack Dulcie when she tried to help her?"

"Lies! All lies! I was standing in the entranceway when it happened. It was a deliberate attack on Irina because she's better than your daughter." She spat out the last words, giving Laura a killing look.

Stunned, the puzzled trainer stood to the side, watching as the quarrel ensued. "I think I'd better call the police," he said at last, slipping away before anyone could stop him.

The story made all the local papers, with Irina's mother proclaiming her daughter's innocence. The trainer washed his hands of the affair by telling both girls he didn't want to work with them again. They could look elsewhere for their figure-skating trainer.

The following Monday, Dulcie dragged herself to school with a reluctant heart. She had only a few not-too-close friends, having spent all her spare time in training, missing parties and dances. Now she thought everyone would avoid her.

So she was really surprised when Emma Blake, the most popular girl in the class, came up to her in the hallway. Emma had snubbed her in the past, belittling her athletic ability. Now Emma was apologetic. "Dulcie, I'm really sorry about what happened. We all know Irina is a bully. You deserve to make the Championships, but I guess this kills your chances, doesn't it?"

All day long kids surrounded Dulcie, offering their sympathy. She felt a warm glow of happiness that eclipsed anything she had ever felt while winning a competition. By the time her mother came to pick her up, she no longer cared about losing her trainer.

Laura put her arm around her daughter. "Your dad and I have decided to move to another city where you can have a fresh start with a new trainer." When Dulcie failed to respond, she asked, "What's the matter, honey?"

"Can't I just skate for fun? Do I have to pursue a gold medal? The most wonderful thing happened today. I made friends with kids who never liked me at all when I was a skating star. Before, when I was winning contests, I felt good about myself, but afterwards I felt empty inside. Mom, I've never even had a boyfriend. I need friends! I think what I really want to do with my life is become a nurse or a therapist. I want to be with other people, helping people. Love and friendship—isn't that what life is all about?"

At that moment, Dulcie saw a new kind of pride shine in her mother's eyes.

PART NINE

A Stitch in Time

Threadbare

Joanne Malley

She sat upon her rocking horse,
Its motion soothed her pain.
Afraid to move, she grabbed on tight
While tears fell forth like rain.

Her tattered dress was floral print
With mangled bows of red,
She fiddled with the dirty lace
And pulled a dangling thread.

A piece unraveled like the seams
That loosened 'round her heart,
If only needles and some thread
Could mend each damaged part.

The fabric of her life's been sewn
By hands that did not love,
Just hurtful words and empty arms
Were all that she knew of.

The pain she reaped was not deserved
Abuse had woven strife,
The patches that were put in place
Could not repair her life.

Neglect had left her heart threadbare
All hope eroded thin,
Her wish to know parental love
Stayed buried deep within.

The time had come to mend the seams
And God now held the thread,
For he would guide the needle through
Each part that once had bled.

He mended all the rips and holes
To blot out all her pains,
He ironed all the wrinkled parts
And banished all the stains.

For not one child should know the life
That she once had to live,
They all deserve the healing touch
That only God can give.

The fabric of her life's been darned
Each thread's secure and tight,
Her Tailor used a special stitch
That made each wrong so right.

For now the pieces of her dress
Are mended, fresh and new,
The rigors of a tattered past
No longer will ensue.

Now more mature with hair of gray
Her mind recalled those days,
With no regrets, she'd change not one,
To God she owes her praise.

He sat upon her rocking chair
And held his precious child,
She gazed upon her perfect dress
And hugged the Lord and smiled.

~ ✤ ~

*Jesus said, "Let the little children come to me,
and do not hinder them, for the kingdom of heaven
belongs to such as these."*
Matthew 19:14

I Learn Something New About Millie

JAN ACKERSON

$\mathscr{I}$ TURN OFF THE EVENING news and reach for my half-solved crossword
puzzle. *Opera tenor Schipa . . .*

The Saturday puzzle is notoriously difficult, but I am determined to finish it.
Millie—my bride of sixty-seven years—teases me about my insistence that each
puzzle be solved completely, in ink. She finds me silly, but there is something
pleasing about the glide of ink on newsprint and a neatly completed black-and-
white grid.

I look away from my puzzle when I hear a small noise from Millie's chair.
She pushes herself slowly upward with an *oof* and shuffles to her sewing room,
one hand on her troublesome hip. When she returns, she is carrying her sewing
basket.

I cherish these quiet evening moments. From outside there is only the
sound of amorous tree frogs; inside, the house holds only echoes of memories. I
return to my puzzle, with an occasional glance at Millie, whose shapely legs can
still make my breath catch in my throat.

She is sewing a button on a shirt that I have not worn in a decade. Her
reading glasses perch low on her nose; nevertheless, she holds the shirt close to
her face and squints with each jab of the needle. Sometimes she puts the shirt
down and flexes her fingers. They must ache—the evening is humid.

I find myself peeved. Why should Millie spend her time in this unnecessary
pursuit? I have more shirts than I need, and I certainly have not missed this one.

Our eyes meet—she smiles—and I return to my puzzle.

Sultanate in Borneo . . .

There are only a dozen blank squares remaining when I'm distracted again
by a soft grunt from Millie's direction. She has finished the shirt and is reaching into her basket for the darning egg and a holey sock. I watch as she begins
to mend the damage, and I feel my guilt and annoyance rise. I should not walk
about the house in stocking feet, but surely we can afford to replace worn socks.

Medial meniscus site . . .

When Millie sighs and massages her neck, I finally decide to speak. Chagrined, I sound like a crabby old man. "Why are you doing that?"

Millie smiles, her cheeks plump and pink. "Doing what, dear?"

I cross over to her and rummage through the basket. "Millie, there are things in here that I haven't worn in years. And this handkerchief—you don't need to mend this! I'll buy you a new one! Your hands hurt, your neck hurts, you can't see without your glasses . . ."

Millie puts her hand on my arm and shushes me. "I've been mending on Saturday evenings for over sixty years. Do you want to know why?" She closes her eyes, and I know that she is composing a little speech. I wait, certain that I'm about to be lectured for my slovenly habits.

"I was so young when we married, Jack, and then you were gone for so long, in the war. I'd join the other Army wives sometimes in the evenings, just for something to do. But you know how shy I am—I took some mending along so I'd have something to look at."

I'm a foolish old man. I believe that's the end of Millie's story. I pick up the newspaper and study the last clue. But Millie's voice interrupts me again.

"You old poop, I'm not done. Do you remember Gloria Bain?"

I nod, remembering Charlie Bain's flame-red hair, and the medics loading his shattered body into their jeep . . .

"She was so mean to me, Jack! She criticized every stitch, and mocked me for mending items that she would have thrown away. I kept sewing just to spite her. And then . . . when she lost Charlie . . . I kept sewing out of contrition." Millie hesitated, her eyes glistening. "I repented years ago, but by that time, Saturday sewing was just a habit. I guess I'm too old to change, now. But—you know what? I hated it when I was young, and I still hate it today. Isn't that ridiculous?"

I stand and take the darning egg from her hand, then kiss her wrinkled cheek. "Sweetheart, it's time to stop. Let me put the basket away for you."

When I return from the sewing room, I see that Millie's expression is bemused. "But Jack—what will I do on Saturday nights?"

I take Millie's hand and lead her to the davenport. "Sit here with me. Do you know a five-letter word for *fabulist*?"

A Thread Unbroken

KENN ALLAN

"*Mommy! Mommy! Come here quick!*"
Implores her frantic shout,
"*I cut the hair on Teddy Bear,*
An' stuffin's fallin' out."

With cocoa and some fuzzy yarn
I mend the wound with care
And pray she'll see no tragedy
Worse than a leaking bear . . .

"*Oh, Mom, I don't know what to do,*"
She moans with tortured face,
"*This gown's too long and fits me wrong*
And I'll look out of place."

I raise the hem with patient sighs
And sense her tensions shrink
As youth is shed like frazzled thread
Of polyester pink . . .

"*Mother, could you lend a hand?*"
Her tone an anxious wail,
"*A rose brocade of heavy suede*
Has tangled in my veil."

My scissors' blades must fully join
Before they draw apart—
I snip the ties with misty eyes
And free her borrowed heart . . .

"Gramma? Can you fix my jeans?"
(I hear his mother speak!)
*"I tore the knees while climbing trees
An' Mom is gonna freak."*

With denim thread and mellow heart
I tread where time has flown,
And thank the LORD for my reward—
To reap what I have sewn.

If Only I Was Dorcas

MELANIE KERR

*L*ET'S SUPPOSE I DIED today. It wasn't a long drawn out affair of gasping breaths and whispered words. It wasn't so swift and surprising like a car accident, that I had no time to prepare. I just became ill and didn't get better. At the end it was like turning off the lights and gently closing the door to this life and falling to sleep. It was a good death.

Let's suppose that I am tucked in my coffin. One would hope that I am wearing my best blue dress. It brings out the blue flecks in my eyes, not that you can tell. I was never one for wearing much makeup, so I hope it is a natural look, not too heavy on the lipstick. I had hoped to touch up the roots on my hair, but never mind.

I hope that the conversation isn't too solemn and hushed. I don't mind a few jokes or some carefully chosen cheerful anecdotes of the things I had done. By all means, wear black if you feel you have to, but try to smile, even just a little. Remember, I have gone to a better place.

Let's suppose that in the next town, not too many miles away, is a church leader. He has been given the keys to the kingdom. The Spirit of God rests upon him powerfully. He reaches down to the lame, pulls them to their feet, and dances with them into the church. When he is arrested for preaching the gospel, an angel is dispatched to unlock the doors and send him on his way. Some say that this man, this church leader, has even walked on water.

Do you send for the man?

If my name was Dorcas, you would have gone to the nearby town to urge him to come at once. She was a disciple who was always doing good and helping the poor.

If I were Dorcas, you would have taken him up to the room where I lay and shown him the clothes I had made. There might have been a wonderful wedding dress that I had carefully sewn together. As I worked in the light of a candle, I would have been praying for the bride-to-be. I would have prayed for a fruitful married life, for fulfilment and harmony, for children and laughter.

Perhaps you show him a simple, strong shirt of a working man. It's nothing dainty or fragile, but fit for the fields and fighting against thistles. As I sewed the seams I would pray that he would be strong to fight the thorns of injustice in the village where he lived.

When you sent for the man, did you expect a noble tribute spoken at my graveside? Did you entertain the possibility of his turning you out of the room, taking me by the hand, and commanding me to awaken?

You see, the community could not function without Dorcas. She had an essential contribution to make and they just couldn't do without her. There was no understudy waiting in the wings to say her lines, no one to pick up the mantle she dropped. She was irreplaceable, so God restored her to her church.

I am not Dorcas. I am not dead yet, but if I was, and if there were such a man in the nearby town, would you call him? Is there anything you could show him about what I have done that was good and helped the poor? There are no wedding dresses, no simple, strong shirts that I have made and given away. What can you show him, what evidence can you provide that I have an essential contribution to make? Can you persuade him that I am irreplaceable?

I cannot be Dorcas. I can only be me.

Is it enough?

❦

Inspired by Acts 9:36-42

Through the Eye of a Needle

Elizabeth Baize

*S*USPENDED BY THE NEEDLE clamp, Flash felt a quiver run down his shaft. Finally, after months of being cooped up in that plastic box, his time to shine had arrived. He recalled, with slight irritation, the teamwork lecture Rusty had given him the night before.

"You must realize you are only *one* of the necessary parts of the entire machine," the older needle had cautioned. "Some of those guys have been a part of the machine since it was new. For example, you'll be working closely with the bobbin case. Listen to his pointers, and I'm sure you'll be sewing in no time. You're a sharp kid, but don't let that go to your head."

"Thanks, Rusty," Flash had quipped, "but remember, only pins have heads."

Rusty had sighed and retired to his pin cushion, leaving Flash to dream of the day that he would make his debut into the sewing world.

And now that day had arrived. The lady of the house would soon commence the construction of her chosen project, and he, Flash, would become a stunning success—a celebrity in the world of needles and sewing machines.

The daydream ended as Flash was jerked into a new position. Why, the lady had just flipped on the power switch. Flash could see her agile fingers slipping a blue thread through the tension and the thread guide. Then he realized that the end of the thread was aimed for his eye. Instinct told him to blink, but better judgment came to his rescue. He would have to put up with the necessary ordeal of being threaded.

Suddenly he was being lowered into a black hole where someone snatched his thread and gave it a tug. Flash was infuriated. "Stop! Who are you and what are you doing?"

Before his eyes could adjust to the darkness, Flash found himself back in the daylight. A chuckle drifted from the hole.

"So, you're new. Son, I'm the bobbin and I just hooked my thread around yours. Now we're set to sew. Just let me catch your thread every time you come down, and you can pull the stitch tight on your way up. Got it?"

Flash gripped his thread at this threat to his independence. "So you're the bobbin I've heard about? Well, just listen, mister, from now on I'll do the sewing for this outfit, and you can just take a break."

At the sound of his own voice, Flash felt his confidence returning. Who needed a bobbin? Rusty and his lectures could just get lost in a haystack.

Flash's eye focused on the folds of blue headed his direction and he hardly heard the response from the hole. "I assure you I won't take a break. But if you keep insisting on your way, it won't be pretty."

The moment had come. As electricity flowed into the machine, Flash plunged through the cloth and once again found himself in the presence of Mr. Bobbin. How dare this impudent fellow capture his thread! He would outmaneuver the nimble bobbin at any cost.

Above the cloth, Flash glanced back at his stitches with satisfaction. He was just preparing for his next dive into the sea of blue when it happened. Rather, nothing happened.

Flash found himself helplessly jammed in position. He could only watch in despair as the agile fingers pulled the cloth from beneath him and been slicing through his stitches with a ripper.

What was happening? He hated to resort to asking, but . . .

"Mr. Bobbin, what's going on?"

"It's just a big tangle down here. I'd rather get some real sewing done if you don't mind."

"You mean I'm not really sewing?" Flash quavered in disbelief.

"Well, son, it takes both of us, plus the whole machine, to form real stitches. Do you want to be a part of the team and work with us? We need you, but you have to be willing to cooperate."

The fingers were placing the material beneath him again as Flash let the bobbin's words sink in. They needed him, but could he accept that he needed them as well?

"I'll give it a try," he called down. As he clenched the first stitch, Flash sensed a new desire to belong. He could work as part of the team.

Reveling in his harmony with the rest of the machine, Flash rose and fell, a row of perfect stitches stretching in his wake.

Keepin' 'em in Stitches

MARILEE WILLIAMS ALVEY

"*T*HIS IS IT—THE final showdown," Satan hissed, gliding sideways. It was no wonder he had been called a serpent. Over the centuries, he was so used to skirting the truth that even his putrid grey-green form had developed a decidedly sideward gait.

"Great Prince of Darkness, why not use some younger demon?" his minion, Bedlam, wheezed as smoke rolled from his cavernous mouth. Sitting on his smoldering haunches, he continued, "Hades knows, you've got enough of 'em now."

"I would, but you don't understand. This is *Mildred*."

"Mildred? Who's she?"

"The most persistent, stubborn bag of bones I've ever seen. If she'd been in Eden, I'd still be talking today and that fruit would be as dried up as she is. Her bill's come due, and I want you, my most foul, to pay her a visit. Her spunk could serve me well."

"Are you serious? A full-frontal attack? I thought with society like it is today our technique is simply to let the world entangle itself on auto pilot."

"I'm as serious as Calvary. This is *Mildred* . . ." The master shuddered, creating an enormous wind as he departed in a powerful slither.

Arriving on Mildred's front porch in the dark of night, Bedlam peered into her window. The frail, gray-haired woman sat in her rocker, stitching by firelight.

Mildred, indeed! His pointed tongue flicked at his perennially parched lips as he imagined the old woman's horror at his countenance.

Sliding under the door with ease, he stood up in his most sinister form and prepared for his heart-stopping entrance. Springing before her, his voice boomed. "Mildred, I am the demon prepared for you before the beginning of time."

"What? My lemon, prepared for me for my tea time?" Mildred asked, unflinching, as she calmly sewed on her quilt.

"Not your lemon," he screamed. "Your *demon*."

"Goodness, you must have been quite a sourpuss for your mother to name you Lemon.

"I have to apologize, Lemon. As I grow older, it seems to me my ears are just shutting down. Please sit down, but, first, could you do me a favor? My nose still works and I smell something burning. Could you check for me and see if I left my oven on?" She continued to stitch, not looking up.

"Old woman, prepare to meet your doom!" he shrieked.

"Yes, I supposed this place could use a broom, but, you know, with my eyesight so poor, it really doesn't bother me anymore."

This Mildred was really getting under Bedlam's leathery skin. Hearing, eyesight, smell, touch, and taste. *Taste won't help here*, he thought. *I even burn water.*

"Mildred," he spoke coyly, "where are my manners? I forgot to shake hands with you when I entered."

"Certainly. My pleasure," she said, extending her hand.

As he grasped it, his yellow eyes gleamed with the expectation of victory.

"Oh, my! These Midwestern winters are killers on the skin. Here," she said, putting some lotion on her hands and rubbing it on his bony, scaly fingers. "I always keep a small bottle here as I sew. I've sewed so much over the years, Lemon, that I'm afraid I've got calluses."

Bedlam's anger raged. A force field of heat surrounded him. This was, indeed, no ordinary human. It was . . . *Mildred.*

He shuddered.

"Oh, my. Is it hot in here to you?" she asked. "I've been having my own personal summers ever since my hysterectomy thirty years ago. Those hormones are still raging."

Bedlam knew how they felt.

"Could you do me a favor, Lemon?"

"Yes?" he hissed.

"Would you mind pointing out where my last stitch ended? My eyes are so weak, and I seem to have lost my place."

"Certainly," Bedlam answered slyly. "It's right here." He pointed to the spot with his tail, waiting for her to trace its scaly form with her fingers.

Belying her years, and, no doubt, with Heavenly help, Mildred quickly stitched the tip of his tail to her quilt. Bedlam yelped and, in his panic, bounded out—sans tail.

Calmly ripping his tail from the material, she threw it into the fire and continued her stitching. "Lord, your plan for the elderly is so wise. Thank you, that you have dimmed my senses so that I can better battle my demons."

Bedlam returned to Satan's lair.
"Yes?" Satan asked, expectantly.
"Suffice it to say, she got my point," Bedlam answered with false bravado, as he bounded out . . . backwards.

Labor of Love

Sandra Petersen

~⤳✦⤲~

SHE HUNCHED OVER A snowy white piece of cotton and lace. On the table beside her, a candle flickered, its flame sputtering low in a pool of tallow. Her eyes burned from the hours spent over her sewing.

From a corner of the room came the rustling sound of bed covers being pushed back and her husband dressing.

She frowned before drawing the needle in and out of the fabric again. *It can't be dawn already. I have so much left to do.*

She glanced around her, only now noticing the light that had seeped in through the curtained window, touching the objects in the room with stony grayness.

"Lydia?" Her husband gently placed a calloused hand on her shoulder. "Please tell me you didn't spend all night on the wee lassie's gown."

Allowing the needle to fall to her lap, she reached to touch his hand. "'Tis a labor of love, Seth. I had to." She strained to look up into his eyes. "I had to," she emphasized.

His eyes softened at her words. "Aye," he mumbled, caressing her cheek before shambling to the door. "They will be here soon. Will ye be ready?"

"Aye," she whispered in reassurance.

He paused for a few seconds, watching as she bent over her sewing. He shook his head and let the door close after him.

They will be here soon. I must be ready. The words echoed in her head.

Her fingers picked up the needle again and drew it through the cloth, attaching the lace to the hem.

She had labored all winter, crocheting the delicate flowered pattern of the lace, envisioning the gown she would construct. As the new life kicked inside her, she cut cloth and began to stitch this tiny dress. Seth busied himself building a cradle. Every minute of work was accompanied by prayer and praise to their Lord and Savior. The baby, a girl she hoped, would be dedicated to the Lord one Sunday in this dress.

Two nights ago the waiting came to an end. The labor began much earlier than expected and with such ferocity that Seth had no time to seek out the midwife. In the midnight hours, she delivered, with only her husband to attend to her needs. She guided his worried movements with her fevered breaths, and when at last it was over, she rested. He bathed the tiny girl and then he, too, slept.

As soon as she mustered the strength, she asked Seth to help her to her rocking chair. At first, he resisted but she hushed his protests.

"Seth, the Lord is our strength and salvation. Our hearts must trust and rejoice in Him. I will finish what I started." Trembling, she picked up the unfinished gown. Her hands became steady as she smocked the bodice and hemmed the sleeves and collar. *A labor of love? Aye, it was.*

She sewed the last frothy bit of lace to the hem and picked up a tiny pearl button from the table top. At the general store, she had bartered fresh eggs for those buttons. A costly decoration, she thought at the time.

As she drew the needle through the shank of the button at the neckline, she pricked her finger. A crimson dot bloomed at her fingertip where the needle pierced. She set her needlework on the table and stood on wobbly legs. Sticking her finger in her mouth, she hobbled to the window and peered out.

The apple tree in the field was abounding with blossoms. They would have a good harvest this autumn. Under the outstretched limbs of the tree, Seth leaned on a shovel, talking with a neighbor. They both glanced toward the sod house, and Lydia withdrew from the window.

Her finger was not bleeding anymore. Mindful of the time, she picked up the tiny gown and finished sewing on the button.

The sound of a wagon and horses drew her attention. She glanced toward the small pine box where their wee daughter slept.

Sleeping now, but we will see you again in Heaven. The Lord promised.

The door opened. "Lydia? Are ye ready? The preacher's here," Seth said, his grief-filled eyes alighting upon her finished work.

She nodded, tears washing her cheeks, and together they dressed their firstborn for her burial.

⤏⊹⤎

Dedicated with love and hope to those parents whose arms ache
for the little one that never drew breath.
We will embrace them in Heaven.

Not a Patch on the Alternatives

Helen Paynter

~⁓⊷✣⊶⁓~

Jesus does not carry a needle and thread.

~⁓⊷✣⊶⁓~

STIFF WITH SELF-IMPORTANCE, the Pharisees laid a cloth before him with haughty hands. It was a tablecloth, richly embroidered through centuries of tradition and custom. Its glowing colors dazzled; its intricacies bewildered.

"Well?" Their narrow eyes challenged him. "Show us where your teachings fit in." Smug in its self-evident perfection, they dared him to point out an inconsistency, a flaw requiring repair.

"I will not," he replied. "The kingdom of God is a new thing. It cannot be patched onto old cloth. It will tear away at the first wash and both will be ruined."

Brimming with success, the scientists spread a collection of cloths before him. At once magnificent yet incomplete, each piece was joined to the next with minute stitches. And emerging from the scraps was a great, beautiful picture of the universe in all its complexity. But there were gaps, places where the puzzle was still incomplete.

"See what we have discovered." Pride was written across their faces. "We would like to do you the honor of inviting you to fill in the gaps. We believe you have much to teach us in these areas of our ignorance."

"I will not," he replied. "I will not tack the truths of the Kingdom into your collage. When you have fresh knowledge, you will discard them like old cloth. "But come, bring them to me and see how they fit into my Father's great picture."

Radiant with political correctness, the people bring before him a patchwork they have made together. Here is every shade, every shape, every tone, cobbled together into a glowing hotchpotch of diversity.

"Add a piece," they urge him, bland goodwill in every expression. "Contribute your own distinctive teaching to this glorious melee."

"I will not," he replies. "I am not one truth among many. I will not present myself on a menu for selection or rejection.

"Bring these pieces to me. See how gladly my Father will receive them, and how they will adorn the fabric of heaven. For my Father's kingdom is rich in diversity, and every tone, every shade, every shape is welcomed there."

Complacent with their lot, the rich offer him their overcoats.

"Something is lacking," they admit with unfamiliar guilt. "Patch your salvation on the sleeve here, so that we will be complete."

"I will not," he replies. "I will not be a band-aid for your lives.

"But remove your overcoats. Come to me in your nakedness, and see how I will clothe you."

Broken, the humble show him their rags. "These are the threadbare remnants of our lives," they confess. "Can you do something to mend them?"

"I will not," he replies. "Why would you want to keep these scraps? And what would they look like if I mended them?

"I will do something new in you. Come to me; lay these tatters aside, and see how I will clothe you. In finest white; in gowns that will never soil. I will dress you fit for the kingdom."

~~⟡~~

Jesus is not in the business of make-do and mend.

A Pot Bellied Proposal

Betty Castleberry

$\mathcal{N}$EXT TO MY SEWING machine, the internet is my favorite thing. That's where I met Johnny, and I wasn't even looking for a man. I was really looking for a recipe for roast pork with capers, and I've never even eaten capers. That Food Network sure gives me funny ideas.

I googled *pig*, and *pork*, and *capers*, figuring that covered it all. Somehow, I got directed to a message board for pot bellied pig owners. Turns out there was a fella there looking for somebody to make a cape for his pet pig, Truman. Seems most folks who own pot bellied pigs spoil them somethin' terrible. Johnny says Truman is smart as a whip, and deserves to be spoiled. He's got him all set up in the house with a bed and a litter box.

Johnny thought Truman would need a cape this winter. I'm not one to brag, but I'm no stranger to a sewing machine. I made all my cousins' bridal gowns, and I make my own clothes, too. Making a little ol' cape would be easy.

Johnny only lived forty miles from me. I knew then that the good Lord had something special planned for us. It couldn't have been just an accident that he lived so close. He could have been from Siberia. Seems peculiar, too, that he was looking for a seamstress, and I just happened to be one.

We set up a time to meet in the park, so I could get Truman's measurements. I told him I'd wear a big, yellow bow in my hair and that-a-way, he'd know me.

I got there first and sat down at a picnic table. Shortly, the prettiest man you ever laid eyes on came walking up with a low-slung, fat, black pig on a leash. It ain't every day you see pampered pork being led around by such a good-lookin' fella.

He nodded in my direction and said that I must be Becca Sue. I said yes I was. He tried to introduce me to Truman, but by then he was rootin' around under the picnic table.

It didn't take long for me to get Truman's measurements, after Johnny coaxed him over to me. We hesitated a good while before we said our goodbyes. Johnny and I, that is. Truman didn't say anything at all.

Johnny asked if I'd like to go for a ride in his Mustang convertible on Friday night, and would I mind if Truman went along? I wasn't crazy about sharing a date with a pig, but I did want to get to know Johnny better, so I agreed.

He showed up on time, and since it was such a nice summer night, the top was down on his convertible. Truman was in the passenger seat. He snorted at me and we had a stare down. I thought I was going to have to ride in the back, but Johnny did make him move.

Riding in that convertible sure was fun. We got a lot of looks with Truman ridin' in the back seat. He had his snout in the air sniffin' the breeze.

We stopped at a drive-in, and Johnny ordered Truman his own Dr Pepper®. I think he loved it, because he squealed real loud. It shocked that snooty banker in the car next to us so bad, he dumped his chocolate malt in his lap. Truman squealed again. What a ham.

I know it ain't Christian, but I laughed. I decided right then I liked Truman.

When Johnny took me home, I got out my sewing machine and worked on Truman's cape. I added some silver studs, and made him a matching hat. It all turned out so cute I had to call Johnny. He came over the next Friday and we put the cape and hat on Truman. He was the cutest pig this side of the Mason-Dixon line.

Johnny called me the next morning. He said he knew it was awful quick, but wondered if I might want to think about stitchin' up another wedding gown. I said I'd think on it, but I knew I'd say yes. Truth is, I wasn't far from being a spinster. Besides that, Johnny is a fine man. The only thing he asked of me is to never serve him pork chops.

I finished my wedding gown, and now I'm sewing the tux for the best man. I know Truman will do it justice.

Silver Needles, Silken Threads

Mid Stutsman

. . . his bride has made herself ready . . .
Revelation 19:7

Antique gold scissors, the silver overlay worn away from centuries of use, snip through silken linen. Silver needles create tiny stitches and a wedding dress takes shape. A song, first formed in my heart, now rises from the depths within.

> *Yards of linen pure and white,*
> *Silver needles, stitches tight,*
> *I will make my dress tonight,*
> *And marry in the morning.*

I hold close the letter from my beloved while I work. My soul rejoices at the eloquent expression of his love, and proposal of marriage. I do not fully understand the sacrifice required of him in order to send it, but with joy I sing, "I am forever yours." I pray he will not tarry.

> *Gathered laces billowing,*
> *Stitched with rosebuds in a ring~*
> *Fair will be my covering,*
> *So lovely in the dawning.*

Ribbons of silk are transformed into delicate rosebuds, capturing the essence of the dawn. I sew them to lace and form my veil. Buttons are covered with satin. Just before sunset, I gather wild rose petals; they will make a fragrant path for my beloved to walk upon.

Silken ribbons overlaid,
Satin buttons I have made.
Fragrant blossoms from the glade,
I'll scatter through the gloaming.

Then a voice, like the sound of a thousand waterfalls, cascades into the timeless pull of love. But it is not the voice of my beloved, and I dare not chase a fleeting dream so close to morning light. For the hour grows late; I must hurry, lest I miss my true love's call.

Fitted bodice, flowing hem,
Swirling layers graced with trim,
I will sew and wait for Him...
His bride I'll be, come dawning.

Long have I labored, struggling to keep myself from wrinkled care—my heart from the sin of doubt. Through it all, the spirit of his love for me, has given me the strength to endure. Now, as I slip into my finished wedding dress, a light breaks forth in the East. I hear his rapturous shout!

Pure white linen without stain,
Fragrant, glowing, free from shame,
Worthy thus, I took His name . . .
And married my love in the morning.

PART TEN

Make a Joyful Noise

Long and Loud

Helen Paynter

"**S**orry about that," David apologized to the assembled sheep. He shouldered the kinnor—it was much too big for him—tilted back his head and began to sing, accompanying himself with hesitant notes on the instrument.

"Baa, baa, black sheep,
have you any wool?
Yes sir, yes sir, three bags—"

For the second time his music was rudely interrupted. A harsh keening rose, hovered steadily like a bird of prey, and then stopped as if strangled.

David stood up, scowling. He turned to the sheep, grouped around him like attentive students before a rabbi, addressing them politely. "Please wait. I will be right back."

Inside, his mother was kneading bread. "Mommy, there's a horrible noise spoiling the music!"

Nitzevet looked up, her eyes weary. "What noise? Can't you go somewhere else to sing?"

"No, Mother. I can't. It's very loud. I think I'd hear it anywhere."

"Well, what sort of noise was it?" She struck the bread with the heel of her hand.

David stood for a moment, his head on one side. Suddenly, without warning, he howled like a banshee, continuing on and on until his breath ran out. His mother jumped briefly, then smiled. "But that's the shofar, David. It'll be sounding all day today."

"But I can't play my music with that horrible noise going on!" He stamped his foot.

"They're practicing for the High Holy Day next week." Nitzevet smothered a smile.

"So why do they have to make that awful noise?" He glared, hands on hips.

Nitzevet dusted off her hands and straightened up. "I think it's the best music of the year. This year, it'll be the best music for fifty years."

"That's rubbish. My music is much better than that."

"Really? What does your music mean?" She raised a quizzical eyebrow.

"What do you mean, Mommy? It's just music."

"Oh no. All the best music says something. The shofar says *salvation*." Sitting down, she drew him nearer.

"Well, I didn't hear any words."

"But it doesn't need words. Listen, in ten days it will be Yom Kippur."

David nodded, his eyes solemn. "That's when the High Priest goes into the Most Scary Place."

"The Most *Holy* Place," she corrected him. "But you're right, it is scary. He goes in to offer a sacrifice for forgiveness. And if He has mercy, Elohim will spare his life and he'll come out to tell us. That's when they blow the Shofar."

"So it's a sort of 'yippee.'"

"Exactly. But this year, it's even more special. This is the fiftieth year."

"The fiftieth year of what?"

"The fiftieth year since the last fiftieth year."

David backed away slightly, and the petulance started spreading across his face again.

"No, listen, David. It's the Jubilee Year. It starts on Yom Kippur, next week. It's a year of freedom."

"What does that mean?"

"It means that slaves go free. Don't you remember Benjamin, last year? His crop failed, and he sold himself to Ehud to pay his debts. When he hears the sound of the Shofar, he'll know he's free."

"Really? Free?"

"Yes. And anyone who owes any money—you know old Hannah? She owes Mordecai a lot of money, but when she hears the sound of the shofar, the debt will be wiped out."

"Wow! So it really is saying something."

"Something very special and important. All the best music does. Now then, do you think you should do something different until they've finished practicing?"

The little boy chewed his lip thoughtfully. "No, I think I'm going to make a new song that says something important. And I'm going to sing it to my sheep."

He marched out, concentration fiercely gripping his face.

An hour later, the bread finally in the oven, Nitzevet crept to the door of the house and stood listening. Sitting with his back to her, David played softly on the kinnor and sang with a clear voice.

> *"I will sing a new song to the Lord*
> *Because he has done wonderful things for us.*
> *He makes it known that he has saved us*
> *Everyone can hear that he is good.*
> *Bring the music of the kinnor before him*
> *And let the shofar blow.*
> *Shout and sing for joy to him*
> *Because he is good and fair."* [1]

David caught sight of his mother and turned around. "If I were king, I'd make every year a Jubilee."

She laughed. "Oh, David. That would take a very special king. And you're just a shepherd boy."

─────

[1] Loosely based on Psalm 98

On the Wings of Praise

MID STUTSMAN

*H*ANGING ABOVE THE MOUNTAINS, a cloud of mist swirls and slowly parts, revealing colors as soft as a pastel summer morn. Light, more brilliant than that of the sun in its zenith, illuminates the air. It shimmers like a glistening veil of sequins and diamond dust, and falls slowly until it drapes my broken body.

> *"Can she hear us, Doctor? Will she come back to us?"*
> *"It's hard to tell at this point. The ordeal of the crash on the mountain pass . . . well, let's just say it's miraculous that she even survived. We'll do all we can for her, but ultimately it's up to her."*
> *"Up to God, you mean . . ."*
> *"Yes, of course."*

The glowing atmosphere dances with waves of haunting, majestic music, floating as though each note is suspended and savored before it is released. The sound wraps around my being and holds me in its embrace—warm inside a cocoon of melodic worship and praise, hovering on the edge of eternity, only barely aware of the life I once knew.

> *"Sweetheart, it's Mom. Can you hear me? I love you. Oh Jesus, sweet Jesus, please bring her back. Please . . ."*

A soft, flowing cadence keeps time to the symphonic refrain seeping into my soul. Within the rhythm of each beat, I feel a transformation overtaking my will. At first I resist; then slowly, purposefully, I yield my heart, my thoughts, my being. The music permeates the fibers of my conscience. I feel drawn to its source.

> *"Doctor, why isn't she responding? It's been six weeks . . ."*

"We are doing all we can, but it may not be enough. The damage is beyond our capabilities. Her body must have time to try to heal on its own. Continue what you've been doing: talking, reading, singing. We don't know how much she can comprehend, but there is hope some of it is getting through."

His Word becomes a molten river overflowing with healing. It fills me and pours through my flesh. Pure and holy thoughts consume me, purging the wounds of a lifetime. Surrounded by angelic praise, I feel only the joy of His presence as I continue to change—corruptible fading into incorruptible.

"Honey? It's been five months. I'm still praying. God knows what's best for you; I know that. And I know He loves you . . . more than I do, even. I just wish you could let me know if you can hear me . . ."

The tempo of the music builds, beckoning. I am aware of a new strength within. The transformation is complete, and I struggle against the constraints of that which has encompassed me within its sacred chambers of harmony and grace. I desperately want to leave and become a part of the sound.

"Doctor?"
"I wish I had good news, but after nine months of hanging on, your daughter can no longer breathe on her own. Her vital organs have shut down. I'm sorry . . . you need to make a decision."
"Please, my angel, it's so hard to think of letting you go. Just let me know somehow that you understand I'll always love you . . ."

My eyes flutter open just long enough to make out the form of my mother kneeling beside my bed, her head bent. I hear her tears of grief and resignation fall like the gentle tinkling of silver chimes upon our clasped hands. I squeeze her hand in response. She looks up, and a thankful knowing floods her eyes as she sets me free.

"Goodbye, my precious. I love you so much . . ."

The veil of light, radiant with gemstone brilliance, parts to reveal the breathless splendor of Eternity. Time is no longer able to hold back the chorus of *Alleluias*, resounding through Heaven's courts. A smile of pure joy graces the mortal shell I must leave behind, and like a butterfly breaking free from its cocoon, I fly on wings of praise into my Savior's waiting embrace.

Author's Note:

I cannot begin to fathom what it must be like to face the heartbreaking decision of whether to sustain the life of a loved one or to set them free to inhabit the perfect realm of Eternity. My heart's desire is that this ministers a measure of peace concerning the matter, and I pray that the Holy Spirit comforts and imparts His wisdom in each case brought before the throne of Heaven.

Blues

Linda Watson Owen

The blues
rolls its mournful, graveled voice,
there in the dust of Delta ways,
there on a' old board porch reachin'
through time's forever.

In a drowsy land as low and dark
as blues itself,
a moan crawls slow
in its roll
onto summer's heavy breath.

A blue voice weaves,
and twines
through locust drone.

A blue voice floats

like smoke summoned to the river's edge,
then nuzzles thick
into the father of river's mighty mud.

A singer sways,
and groans,
and births a thousand years into
a song,
a thousand tears
into blue.

Wailin'
is the voice that yearns,

alone

in its night of thickening heat
and glistening sweat
on a' old board porch in the Delta.

Sing, blues,
sing,
and show all God's children how to cry.

I say,

Sing, blues, and let your trouble song

float up

up high to Heaven's porch
on the banks of Sinless Sea.

Moan to the Father of Rivers,
and let Him hear your heart birthing
a thousand tears.

Blues.

Let your blues weave with the hue of Heaven
shining through,
shining through God's buzz of star song.

The Father of Rivers embraces the blues,

when it carries you.

Grace Notes in a Minor Key

LINDA GERMAIN

I CURL UP IN A secluded window seat in order to see the big oak tree down by the road. The incessant rain falls like giant tears from sad clouds and blurs my vision. My restless fingers trace the rivulets on the cold pane as I try in vain to find a pattern.

This sturdy old house was built when padded seat nooks were standard, when people took time to be quiet and read, or like me, to gaze into a vague and foggy future while chased by bitter memories of loss, always hoping for some clue to a solution; always hoping for a rescue.

None ever comes.

The oak tree has no leaves. I want to believe it is trembling from exposure to the raw winter weather. How does it go on, year after interminable year, and still burst forth in the spring with an umbrella of new greenery that reaches heavenward for the sustenance of light? The eternal questions in my tortured mind are exhausting.

After my old life crumbled into non-existence, my sister and her husband offered me sanctuary here in the country until things begin to make sense again. They have three children who spend most of their time on the other side of the cavernous house. I hardly ever hear them. From this third floor retreat I pass the endless hours alone. There is a small kitchenette so I am not obligated to join them for meals. My very appreciated private quarters are a temporary cocoon, a safe haven.

Sometimes I try to express my erratic feelings by painting or writing, but it does not give me comfort or relief. The joy I once had in my well-ordered life is now reduced to incapacitating pain. The music in me has withered and died. I can't even pray.

As my eyes strain to make out the shape of the oak, there is a crash of thunder that rattles the glass between the stormy outside and me. Exquisite lightning explodes in a breathtaking kaleidoscope; beautiful, yet terrible. In one devastating second it seeks out the solid and dependable old tree and attacks it without mercy. Huge parts of it fall to the ground in flames until the dousing rain turns fire to smoke.

I gasp in disbelief. "How dare you?" I holler, shaking my fist at the unrepentant sky. "What did that wonderful oak ever do to you?" I have so aligned myself with its steadfastness day after day it never occurred to me it would not always be standing like a sentry at the gates of this lovely home.

I can't seem to stop screaming in rage. "Why did you leave me? I thought you would be there forever like you promised. You have hurt me to my very core. I hate you! I love you! I am lost. Oh God, where are you?"

My kind and patient sister stands nearby with the healing balm of understanding. She knows my purging meltdown has nothing to do with the oak tree. After my anger is spent, I put both hands over my swollen eyes and wait for something I cannot articulate. She sits close and ever so gently wraps her loving arms around me. I can hear the satisfying tenor of congenial voices downstairs. She has left the door open.

When the rain stops, I sit up straight and gaze into her precious face, so like Mama's at that age. I know I am in the right place to begin to reconnect, to fill the emptiness, and to find the music that has deserted my soul.

With quiet strength, she leads me toward the steps to where the warmth of home begins to thaw my protective facade. I am acutely aware of a soothing sound that makes its way to these tone-deaf ears. It is the clear voice of her four-year-old. He is singing; an endearing thing he does unconsciously as he plays.

The pure sweetness in the tune floats upward and washes over my shattered heart. The simple song is all the more effective by his lisp. "Jethuth loveth me thith I know, for the Bible tellth me tho. Little oneth to Him belong; they are weak but He ith thtrong . . ."

A sliver of hope tiptoes in to plant a tiny seed. Tomorrow, when the sun comes out, I want to check on the tree. It's roots go deep, and like me, it just may have survived the storm.

But tonight, I need to listen to a child.

Heart Song

Elizabeth Baize

My roaming feet had led me far
Into the forest glade,
When distant music touched my ears
And did my soul pervade.

Enthralled, I searched to find the source
Of such a joyful song.
'Til all at once I saw a stream
Leap joyfully along.

The glinting waters curled and swirled
Releasing bubbling notes.
The music filled the air as full
As near one hundred throats!

Who could the stream be singing for?
It wasn't just for me.
I'd just arrived upon the scene
To hear the stream so free.

And then to add to questions
That the singing stream did spark,
A flash of yellow caught my gaze
And drew it to a lark.

Upon a branch he bowed and rocked
Until as if on cue,
He let his song float on the breeze
As my own wonder grew.

For why and how could this small bird
Make music rare and sweet,
Arranged with every note in place
To make the song complete?

And then as if to lead me on
The breeze played on the grass,
And whispered such a fragile tune
No other could surpass.

"Why do you sing?" I cried aloud.
"And who gave you your song?"
As nature seemed to then burst forth
In concert sweet and strong.

"At last you've voiced the question
That I longed to hear you raise."
I spun around to face the One
And knelt beneath His gaze.

"I gave each song you've heard today.
And nature heeds my voice
By singing praise at my command
To point you to a choice."

"Will you continue listening
To nature's poignant plea
And only praise its song alone
Without a thought for Me?"

"Or will you look beyond the stars
That sing with one accord,
And choose to sing the song I give
As praises to your Lord?"

In awe I listened to His words
And knew beyond a doubt
I longed to sing to this great King
Eternity throughout.

"Oh Lord," I cried, "my life is Yours.
Your glory fills my gaze."
He smiled, reached out, and filled my heart
With melodies of praise.

A song so new burst from my lips
To glorify my King.
But then I knew what pleased Him most
Was that my heart could sing.

Inspired by:
Job 38:7; Psalm 19:1-3; Psalm 40:3;
and Romans 1:20

Even If . . .

Pat Guy

THE DEATH SONG HAD begun. Every instrument known to man performed its melodious part in celebration to please the king . . . and jubilant he was on this day of dedication. Ninety feet of gold reflected his image for miles toward the horizon. A beacon of pride; a beacon of warning for citizens and travelers alike—on the plains of Dura and in the province of Babylon, the greatest kingdom in the world.

The music played on—harps, lyres, flutes, and zithers. Master musicians quaked in fear of releasing one discordant note, and there were three administrators who trembled at the harmonious beauty that filled their ears and heart, for it would be their last song to hear.

Government officials of all levels had been summoned, and the decree had been heralded throughout the provinces: "O peoples, nations and men of every language, as soon as you hear the sound of all kinds of music, you must bow down and worship the golden image. Whoever does not will be immediately thrown into the blazing furnace."

Standing among the miles of bodies prostrate before the lustrous image, Shadrach, Meshach, and Abednego were immediately summoned before an angry king.

"Is it true," the king seethed, "that you do not serve my gods or worship my image of gold? Fall now and worship the image I made!"

The music played on—harps, lyres, flutes, and zithers, resonating in the palace walls, reminding the men of their faith and strengthening their stand before the king. The chill of fear lifted with each breath of prayer.

Peace loosed their tongues. "O Nebuchadnezzar, we do not need to defend ourselves before you. If we are thrown into the furnace, our God is able to rescue us from your hand. But even if He does not, we will not serve your gods or worship your image."

Royal fury bellowed its indignation. "Soldiers! Tie them up! Heat the furnace seven times more! Now!"

Tongues of fire leaped and lapped at the furnace walls—the crackling whip of Hades reached out and consumed the king's strongest soldiers as Shadrach, Meshach, and Abednego fell from the grips of dead men into the pit.

The king's eyes gleamed and waited . . . Gleamed and . . .

He leaped to his feet and exclaimed above the roaring wind of fire, "Weren't there three men firmly tied? Look! I see four men walking around unbound and unharmed, and the fourth looks like a son of the gods!"

The music played on . . . and the word spread.

Fear could not keep the king from stepping over still-smoldering bodies to reach the opening of the blazing furnace, not questioning why he, himself, was not consumed. "Shadrach, Meshach, and Abednego, servants of the Most High God, come out! Come here!"

Not a hair on their heads was singed, not a hem of their robes was scorched, nor was the smell of fire upon them.

Wonder transcended all peoples, nations, and men of every language.

Then Nebuchadnezzar said, "Praise be to the God of Shadrach, Meshach, and Abednego, who has rescued His servants. They trusted in Him, even if they were to give up their lives to serve only Him. No people of any nation or language shall say anything against their God."

Murmurs ceased and all turned toward the fiery furnace, where three men had been destined to die . . . where the Son of God walked . . . where He set the men free.

The plains of Dura, in the province of Babylon—the greatest kingdom in the world—were silent.

~ ⚜ ~

Based on Daniel Chapter 3

Musical Stirrings

BETH MUEHLHAUSEN

Sing Your song, Singer.
Sing Your love song to me.

Sing through the white caps' *shush-hushing, churn-burning.*
Inspire me to finish the race,
to run and not grow weary.

Sing through the red-winged blackbirds' trills.
Soothe my weariness;
fill my heart with the harmony of heaven.

Sing through the oak leaves' *crack-crackling*
in the canopy overhead.
Protect and shelter me: *rus-rustle, shhhhhhh.*

Sing through staccato raindrops' pattering on the cabin roof.
Exhort me with the drilling urgency
of a whole orchestra of drumsticks.

Sing as if tomorrow will never come,
As if today might suddenly vanish,
As if I might come home to You before the sun sets.
Sing because I long to hear Your promise of hope.

Sing in my heart,
Your strength to impart;
Sing me a psalm,
Your healing balm.

Sing to my tears,
sing to my fears;
sing with the music of the spheres.

Sing your song, Singer.
Sing Your love song to me.

Allelu

JAN ACKERSON

⟵⟶

ALMOST FROM THE DAY he was born, my little Jesus' face has at times taken on a look of intense, calm concentration. Even as an infant, he would often still the flailing of his tiny arms and legs and gaze about, quietly, from his cradle. I always wondered at such times—*what are you thinking, precious one?*

And now he is two years old, and he delights me every day with a new word, a fresh utterance in his childish lisp. I never tire of watching him; he sits and plays with the little Noah's ark that Joseph has carved for him, babbling his version of animal noises and occasionally chastising a wayward bear or lion.

This morning, I was preparing bread for the day and listening to Jesus as he prattled with his wooden animals. When he suddenly fell silent, I looked to the corner where he played and saw that he had that same look again—quiet, serene, with a hint of a smile.

He padded over to me on chubby feet and tugged on my garment, looking earnestly into my eyes. "Music, Mama," he said. "Music."

I stopped kneading the dough and listened, thinking perhaps that a traveling musician was at our gate, playing his lyre in hopes of receiving a bite of fish or a silver coin. I heard nothing but the ever-present locusts, whose raucous complaints could hardly be called music.

"Mama!" Jesus held up his arms, and who could resist such an invitation? I lifted him to my hip and kissed his dark curls. One kiss was enough—he squirmed to get down and toddled to the window with a grin. "Music, Mama!"

There are many things that I do not understand about my little boy, and with every passing day, I feel him slipping out of my arms and into his Father's world.

What music do you hear, my son, that is hidden from my ears?

Creator, You dwell with us now,
And so we proclaim with one voice—
Each creature and each blade of grass,
Each rock and each river—Rejoice!

Allelu, bless Your name, allelu,
Creation is singing for You.

O hear now the animals' choir:
Vicuna, raccoon, chimpanzee—
We offer our song to the King:
Great elephant, tiniest flea.

Allelu, bless Your name, allelu,

Creation is singing for You.
We sing, too. (You only can hear).
The cedars and lilies, the wheat,
Bamboo, passionflower, and palm:
Hosannas we lay at Your feet.

Allelu, bless Your name, allelu,

Creation is singing for You.
A wee grain of sand, and this stone,
This boulder, this mountain, this star—
Our melody will not be stilled,
We glory in all that You are.

Allelu, bless Your name, allelu,
Creation is singing for You.

Come, waters of earth, raise your song:
Murmuring brook, rushing waterfalls, too,
Lake, river and pond, mighty sea,
All join in the great "Allelu!"

Allelu, bless Your name, allelu,
Creation is singing for You.

C Sharp

SANDRA PETERSEN

𝒯HE OPENING STRAINS OF *I Surrender All* floated up to the rafters of the sanctuary. I lifted my clarinet to my mouth and waited.

"Are you tired of wrestling with the Lord, trying to get Him to agree with you rather than agreeing with Him? I invite you to come forward, lay yourself on that altar of submission and surrender to Him. He is waiting for you." The pastor paused. "As the worship team plays, come and give it all to Him."

Pastor nodded at me, my cue to begin. I was to play the entire piece twice as a solo. On the third time through, the vocalists would add their voices, sweetly, softly, as if angels' wings were caressing the souls of the congregation. The tempo was slow and the mechanics of the piece simple enough that I should have no problems.

The notes I played glistened with emotion. As I coaxed the music from my clarinet, my instrument wept with a voice of surrender.

I scanned the congregation for reactions. Some, with eyes closed, stood with hands lifted to the heavens. Old Mrs. Stauffer, her white hair combed into a neat bun, smiled faintly, lost in memories of eighty years of camp meetings and altar calls. Sam and Becky, a young newlywed and newly-saved couple, left their seats to come forward, their faces moist with tears. The leader of the worship team caught my eye and smiled in approval. I wondered why only two people responded, but I figured the chorus would beckon the others.

Then it happened: the dilemma every musician faces at least once in their lives. An instrument malfunction. I pressed the C-sharp key for the first and highest note of the chorus and nothing came out.

Not now. I groaned inwardly.

The C-sharp appeared twice in the chorus, sustained notes both times, and I could not play it.

If this happened during practice, I would scan my clarinet for the culprit, usually a loose pad. When I found it, I would apply the flame of a lighter under the key to get the glue on the pad to adhere again. But my lighter was tucked away in my case, which was under the pew. My husband sat beside it, frowning with concern at the second missed note.

My cheeks blazed with an embarrassed flush. The second time through the piece, I decided to drop the chorus an octave to avoid the malfunctioning key. As I came to the end of the solo, I also came to the end of my clarinet's range. The last two notes were too low for my instrument.

The vocalists began to sing as I held my clarinet in frustration and silently fumed. *I blew it, Lord. I wanted to move more people to come and commit themselves to You, and I couldn't do it.*

His voice whispered to me from within. "No, *you* couldn't. Do you not know the Holy Spirit brings them to Me? Not you. Surrender your musical gift to Me, and I will work through you to move mountains."

My heart wept at His words. Then He added, "Come to the altar, daughter. And bring your clarinet."

Cradling my instrument in my arms, I joined the large group in front already singing, "I surrender all."

My Peace

MELANIE KERR

I will not call him
I will not speak out his name
And summon him to my side
I will not take the peace he offers

His lyre is in my hands now
I will play his songs
My fingers will pick out his melodies
But, elusive, I cannot hold them

This lyre sings for him
Why does it groan in my hand?
Soft notes sigh for him
For me they jangle and jar

His melodies usher in peace
He opens the door to stillness
His music comforts me
And my soul is restored

Without him
Anguish steals though the door
Comfort is absent
And distress overpowers me

I wrestle with the strings
There is only noise
No sweet songs
To lift my fallen spirit

Why must my peace
Rest in his hand?
Each time my heart betrays me
Falling under his spell

David, my servant, my son
He slays giants with a stone
He slays thousands with a sword
He slays demons with a harp

His name is on my lips
I shout, "Come quickly!"
And when he plays
My heart will find rest

I lay down his lyre
And grasp a spear
I will claim back my peace
Even with his blood.

Meet Our Authors

Simple Pleasures Contributors

ALLISON EGLEY lives in the St. Louis, Missouri, area with her family. She works as a Vocational Rehabilitation Intake Specialist. Allison started writing for pleasure in college, and hopes to continue this hobby as long as the Lord allows.

AMY MICHELLE WILEY's love for words and people has led to her work as a writer and editor, and as a sign language interpreter. She has a passion for helping new writers along the journey to publication www.sparrowsflight.com

ANN GROVER lives on a 26,000 acre ranch in northeastern British Columbia, Canada, where her imagination is inspired by her avid interest in history and country life. When not assisting with ranch work, she enjoys photography, reading, baking, and spoiling her three adorable granddaughters.

BETH LABUFF lived most of her life surrounded by the cornfields of Adair County, Iowa, before moving with her husband to northern Arizona. Many of her poems have a rural flavor.

BETH MUEHLHAUSEN lives on the shore of a beautiful lake in southwest Michigan where she enjoys her ever-expanding family, advocates with chronically ill friends in the areas of nutrition and wellness, and writes daily as a form of therapy.

BETTY CASTLEBERRY lives in west Texas with her husband, three parrots, and a dog.

CASSIE MEMMER was a loving wife, caring mother and avid writer. She loved singing praises to her Lord and now spends her time worshiping in His very presence.

CORINNE SMELKER has, at a various times, called three continents and several countries home. Despite that, she is a country girl at heart who loves nothing better than to train and ride horses and walk through the woods observing nature. When not at her computer, writing and editing, she can generally be found out and about with her family, having fun, and enjoying the life the Lord has blessed her with.

DAVID STORY is the Associate Pastor at Second Baptist Church, Pasadena, Texas, and a student at the College of Biblical Studies in Houston. He and his wife Lynette live in Pasadena.

DEBBIE ROOME has been writing since the age of six and has won many awards over the years. She loves to write heartwarming stories that show God's love in action.

DEBORA DYESS lives in Central Texas with her husband, surrounded by friends, children and grandchildren. She is a writer and editor for *'Tween Girls, God eMagazine*, and several other books and short stories.

DOLORES (DEE) STOHLER lives in Colorado Springs where she looks out her front window at the scenic beauty of the Rocky Mountains. Dee and her husband Don have four children, nine grandchildren, and three great-grandchildren, all of whom they love dearly. Dee is a prolific poet and writes with passion.

ELAINE TAYLOR is a housewife who lives in Columbus, Ohio, with her wonderful husband Wally and their beloved pets.

ELIZABETH BAIZE currently lives in Chandler, Arizona. She enjoys finding time to improve her photography, hiking, and riding horses.

ERIN BRANNAN is a wife and mother to four beautiful children. She also owns a professional portrait studio in Denver, Colorado.

GREGORY KANE wrote the story that appears in this book while on missionary service in Africa. He and his family have since returned to the United Kingdom where he works as a church minister.

HELEN CURTIS is the mother of three boys and lives in Adelaide, South Australia. Whilst she isn't so keen on housework, she loves being a stay at home mother to her boys. Helen has a strong faith in God, and reminds herself to hold on to what she knows, not what she feels when things get tough. She knows she is loved by God and her family, and that she has a purpose in life.

HELEN PAYNTER is a part time Baptist minister and fills her spare time doing doctoral work on humor in the book of Kings. She lives in Bristol, England, with her husband and their three daughters.

HOLLY JENSEN is a jill-of-all-trades—singer, podcaster, artist, techy, and of course, writer. She lives in California with her family and her dog, all of whom she loves to pieces.

JAMES CLEM writes occasionally when the mood hits him. He lives in Roanoke, Virginia, with his wife Anna (his personal editor and #1 encourager) along with a handful of pets of all shapes and sizes.

JAN ACKERSON is a retired schoolteacher who lives in rural Michigan. Her greatest joys are her two granddaughters and traveling with her husband. Jan has a passion for peace, justice, and compassion in the Church.

JANET BANNISTER is mother to three girls. She loves the Lord and is passionate about reading and writing.

JOANNE MALLEY is a published writer and creative being at heart. She is married to her long-time sweetheart, enjoys yoga, designing jewelry, and spending time at the beach. Joanne's little words of wisdom are a constant blessing to those who read them.

JOE HODSON lives in Columbus, Ohio, with his wife and two young daughters. He is involved in his local church and other Christian ministries. Joe writes for fun and to glorify the Lord.

KAREN ELENGIKAL is a published author who lives with her husband and six sons in Sydney, Australia. Aside from her passion for writing and photography, Karen's family ministry focus is World Missions, with her family frequently travelling to India and the Pacific Islands, bringing revival and visitation to local indigenous churches. Pastor Karen can be contacted by email: freshdailymanna@tpg.com.au

KENN ALLAN currently resides in the American Pacific Northwest with his wife/editor, their youngest daughter, three precocious grandchildren, and an undisclosed number of cats.

LARRY ELLIOTT lives in rural Arkansas with his wife Pam, two Chihuahuas, and a Great Dane. His dream is to spur the imagination and spirit of young people and adults with awe-inspiring fiction stuffed with the irrefutable truth and wonders of our Creator.

LAURIE GLASS is the creator of Freedom from Eating Disorders, at www. freedomfromed.com, where she provides Christian resources for those in eating disorder recovery.

LINDA GERMAIN is an award winning freelance writer and editor. Poetry or prose, her creative style runs the scale from funny to serious . . . and usually with an interwoven message.

LINDA WATSON OWEN lives and writes in the USA's sunny South. Her award winning poems delight and inspire readers of all ages. Linda welcomes readers to contact her through Facebook or email at lowen72@yahoo.com.

LOREN T. LOWERY lives just north of Seattle, Washington. He tips his hat to God who has blessed him with a loving wife and children, two horses, a rescue dog, and a cat born in his hay barn.

LORI OTHOUSE is a wife, mom, Compassion International advocate, and Sunday School teacher. She is passionate about helping those less fortunate and using words for good, not evil.

LYDIA PATE lives in Yukon, Oklahoma. In the gritty soil of life, she loves to unearth God-moments—diamonds in the rough that can be polished with words to ultimately reveal Jesus.

MARILEE WILLIAMS ALVEY lives in Bloomington, Illinois. She lost her husband to cancer three years ago, but states that he now simply works at the Home Office, while she remains a writer on foreign assignment.

MARTY WELLINGTON lives on the Kansas prairie and writes about the endless wonders she finds there. She is the mother of three girls and has been married for thirty years. Visit Marty at thebeginningofwonder.blogspot.com/

MELANIE KERR teaches in a local high school. She and her husband live in Inverness, Scotland. Melanie has been writing poetry, short stories, and devotionals for a number of years. She has recently published a collection of poetry entitled *Wider Than the Corners of This World*.

MID STUTSMAN is an award-winning author, artist, and photographer, who lives with her husband along the shores of western Lake Michigan, and on their northern Indiana farm. The inspiration for her writing is God's amazing grace, and you can visit Mid's website at www.midspoint.com

MO L. has had her work published both in print and online. Her story in *Simple Pleasures* was based on an account of a long ago shipwreck.

MYRNA NOYES loves to write short stories, with allegories being a favorite type. The whole creative process is exciting and satisfying to her.

PAT GUY believes there is always more to the story, so she enjoys writing that story. She lives in Florida with her husband of over thirty-five years, who comes first in her life—after the dogs.

PATTY WYSONG says life is never dull when you juggle being a wife, mom to a handful of kids and a couple of Capuchin monkeys, life on the road, and being a writer. She clings to the promise that God will enable her to do what He asks of her. You can find her blogging at PattyWysong.com.

ROBYN BURKE likes to say she is living faithfully, loving fully, and laughing freely. It has become her personal testimony as she writes about these truths and the hope found in Christ. You can find examples of this on her blog: burkemissiontravels.blogspot.com.

SALLY HANAN is an Irish import who spends her days strategizing, laughing, and being a general busybody. She currently switches roles as an editor, counselor, and life coach between her two businesses: inksnatcher.com and morethanbreathing.com

SANDRA PETERSEN has been writing fiction and non-fiction since 2006. When she is not busy writing, she gardens, crochets, goes camping, reads, homeschools and takes care of the home she shares with her husband, youngest daughter, and family dog Kiba.

STEPHANIE BULLARD has been writing since she was eight, and by the grace of God will continue to do so until the day she dies. She is an author by heart, but a special education teacher to pay the bills. She lives in Springfield, Ohio with her dogs, Vala and Deeks, and is an active member of her search and rescue team in Columbus.

TABIATHA TALLENT is a pastor's wife and Sunday School teacher in Georgia. She enjoys spending time with her family and friends and is looking forward to the birth of her first grandchild. It is her desire to encourage her brothers and sisters in Christ through her writing.

TAMMY BOVEE, like many brides, walked down the aisle with a heart full of fairytale expectations. Four years into her marriage, Tammy's husband Jeff lost his job and plunged into debilitating depression. She has since let go of her "fairytales" and embracef her real life marriage to Jeff—a love money can't buy.

TERI WILSON is a novelist for Harlequin Books who loves poetry, romance, dogs, books, and dancing every day. Visit Teri at her website: teriwilson.net.

T.F. CHEZUM has been writing poems and stories since childhood, and says that writing is an emotional release.

VERNA COLE MITCHELL is an author who draws from her rich heritage of faith and family to inspire, entertain, and bring a smile. She has two published books of poetry: *Don't Frighten the Pansies* and *Somewhere Beyond the Blue*.

WILLIAM PRICE enjoys writing and the opportunity to draw his readers' attention to the hope we have in the Lord.

MIXED BLESSINGS

Classically Inspired

COMING OCTOBER 2014

#MixedBlessings #ClassicallyInspired

CPSIA information can be obtained at www.ICGtesting.com
Printed in the USA
LVOW08s0702050814

397559LV00001B/5/P